Drogenkonsum in Geschichte und Gesellschaft

Drug Use in History and Society

Herausgegeben von | Edited by
Prof. Dr. Heino Stöver
Dr. Ingo Ilja Michels

Band | Volume 3

Ingo Ilja Michels | Heino Stöver [Eds.]

Drug Treatment, Culture and Social Policy in Central Asia and China

 **Nomos**

The **Deutsche Nationalbibliothek** lists this publication in the
Deutsche Nationalbibliografie; detailed bibliographic data
are available on the Internet at http://dnb.d-nb.de

ISBN   978-3-8487-8711-1 (Print)
         978-3-7489-3102-7 (ePDF)

British Library Cataloguing-in-Publication Data
A catalogue record for this book is available from the British Library.

ISBN   978-3-8487-8711-1 (Print)
         978-3-7489-3102-7 (ePDF)

Library of Congress Cataloging-in-Publication Data
Michels, Ingo Ilja | Stöver, Heino
Drug Treatment, Culture and Social Policy in Central Asia and China
Ingo Ilja Michels | Heino Stöver (Eds.)
142 pp.
Includes bibliographic references.

ISBN   978-3-8487-8711-1 (Print)
         978-3-7489-3102-7 (ePDF)

Onlineversion
Nomos eLibrary

1st Edition 2022
© Nomos Verlagsgesellschaft, Baden-Baden, Germany 2022. Overall responsibility
for manufacturing (printing and production) lies with Nomos Verlagsgesellschaft mbH
& Co. KG.

Introduction: National drug discourses

Ingo Ilja Michels and Heino Stöver

Central Asia (CA) and China are key regions for the international activities tackling illicit drug trafficking and related problems, such as dependence – specifically the problems with illegal opioids, infectious diseases, and increasingly, also synthetic cannabinoids and stimulants (especially methamphetamines in China). The drug phenomena challenge the authorities of state institutions, the social cohesion of the society, the public health and the security of public life. The fact that the "Northern Route" with trafficking heroin, morphine and opium towards Russia and Europe crosses CA has made that region not only vulnerable to drug trafficking, but – increasingly – also to local drug consumption. Central Asian countries (Kazakhstan, Kyrgyzstan, Tajikistan, Turkmenistan, Uzbekistan) are experiencing drug related problems, such as a high prevalence of drug dependence and the threat of infectious diseases such as HIV/AIDS and hepatitis among injecting drug users (with a high prevalence of 4–20 % respectively 60–80 %). The same is true for China. Although both in Central Asia as well as in China the prevalence of consumption of those substances has decreased in the last years, not at least due to effective measures of prevention, treatment and harm reduction. All countries in Central Asia and China are supporting the common view of the UN bodies (UN Drug Convention 1961, Art. 38 and Political Declaration 2009) to implement all practicable measures for "prevention, early identification; treatment, education, after-care and rehabilitation and social reintegration" of drug dependent people. According to the "UNGASS Political Declaration from 1998" all Member States are firmly bound to "respect of human rights, fundamental freedoms, dignity of individuals and equality" and agreed on the general principles of drug policy, such as an "integrated, multidisciplinary, mutually reinforcing and balanced approach; a common and shared responsibility and increased international cooperation".

Modern and effective approaches to treat drug use disorders, according to the UN/WHO International Treatment Standards, exist in all countries but lack institutionalisation and require further scaling-up and harmonisation. NGOs, an important part of efficient and sustainable drug policies, are weak in all countries and lack the basis of work.

However, drug dependence is still seen more as a problem of "social deviance" in both Central Asia and the China than as a treatable disease; repressive drug laws, registration systems mean that many of those affected face long prison sentences and that the police and judiciary are not cooperating adequately with health services. This promotes the social exclusion of those affected.

Of increasing importance is the support of the *education of social work* in the Central Asian countries and in China, which in Europe and especially in Germany plays a central role in the prevention and treatment of drug dependence and its health and social consequences. But social work as a means of reducing these problems is still in its infancy in both Central Asia and China, although the positive role of social work is now increasingly recognized on a socio-political level.

The program of the EU "Central Asian Drug Action Program" (CADAP) is about "the establishment of functional and effective treatment and harm reduction programs based on EU and international standards (which) are essential to provide the best and cutting-edge health responses, programs and models to CA countries' populations. This output will focus on strengthening demand reduction models on the basis of best EU and international practices for harm reduction, rehabilitation and social reintegration, and therapeutic communities." (Annual Action Document 2019 for the program in favour of the Central Asia region; July 2019). The Frankfurt University of Applied Sciences had been responsible for the implementation of the focus "Treatment" in the 5th and 6th phase of the program and has decades of expertise in the training of social work in Faculty 4 "Social Work and Health" (Bachelor, also a course "Social Work: transnational" and the Master's course "Addiction Therapy and Social Management in Addiction Help") and in practical research, in particular through numerous research projects of the project manager Prof. Dr. Heino Stöver and the research stay of Dr. Ingo Ilja Michels from 2006 and 2008 in the People's Republic of China to accompany and support the development of an opiate substitution program including social work (especially with a model character in Shanghai).

The *Exceed Program* of the German Academic Exchange Service (DAAD) to support Excellence Centres for Exchange and Development was first launched in 2009 with the aim of bringing together the involvement of German higher education institutions and their partners in developing countries and raising its public profile. The initiative also aims to institutionalize research and teaching cooperation between higher education institutions in Germany and in countries of the Global South more accessible to development cooperation.

The program "Social work and strengthening NGOs in development cooperation to treat drug addiction" (SOLID) of the Frankfurt University of Applied Sciences is a jointly developed research program on the influence of social work on the prevention and treatment of drug addiction with the main focus on role of NGOs. The program was developed in cooperation with universities that teach social work/social medicine in Kazakhstan, Kyrgyzstan, Tajikistan, Uzbekistan and the People's Republic of China. Central Asia/China is confronted with a growing drug problem. Social work with drug dependents is not offered either in university training or in practice. The well-being of those affected also depends on the psychosocial support offered and the reduction of stigmatization and marginalization, so that social work measures in particular represent an important component in dealing with this. The research project builds on previous research projects of the Institute for Addiction Research (see also CADAP and InBeAIDS; see: Stöver, Michels 2022), which have already produced successful cooperation and important results in cooperation with the participating countries in Central Asia. The research project aims at a professional exchange between German and the Central Asian/Chinese partner universities, and is based on SDG goals (Sustainable Development Goals) in the context of improved development cooperation – in particular Goal 3 Health and well-being ("Health is a goal, a prerequisite and result of sustainable development") and 4 high-quality education ("In post-Soviet Central Asia, as well as in China, high-quality (training) education is an important socio-political concern. However, there are too few specific training opportunities in the field of prevention and treatment of addictions ") and strives to strengthen university cooperation in and between these countries. The participating universities/research institutions will sharpen their professional profile in teaching and research in line with the 2030 Agenda. In the long term, graduates will be qualified to take on positions of responsibility through their studies in practice-oriented and state-of-the-art courses in "Social Work" (or related terms, for example in the health sector).

The Research program is focussed on the following assumptions:

Classical definition of social work in drug treatment work, such as supporting patients and building bridges to families, relatives, employment etc. in order to stabilize patients vs. more critical perspectives on recovery and drug treatment. How is classical social work in addiction treatment reflected in Western and Eastern treatment models? What is the history of drug treatment from medicalization to psycho-social support to harm reduction and individual choice? What are critical perspectives on a neoliberal agenda and its implication in harm reduction, international drug control apparatus, the UN and global drug policy? Regarding the organization of detox – how does global drug policy affect the implementation of day-to-day social work practice in each country? What are the consequences of zero-abstinence policies on immediate intervention – detox, and following care i.e. psycho-social support? How are different kinds of drugs addressed in different treatment schemes? What is the purpose of detox in each country? Where are the overlaps and differences in both philosophy of treatment and the implementation? What is the social construction of dependence in the different countries, within cultural contexts, and the perception of the nature of the disease? Where does care come from? Who can help people who are seeking treatment? How do local implementation strategies reflect the global order of drug control as well as local contexts? (Lasco 2022)

The expected results of the research cooperation will contribute to the establishment and expansion of regional networks. At the same time, the expertise within the framework of university responses to the problem of drug addiction/therapy is intended to strengthen the health discussion in these states, including politics and civil society (especially NGOs).

In this edition we present first thoughts on the development of the treatment of drug addicts and the role of social work in it are presented by the scientists of the partner universities, who fill a postdoc position in the SOLID project.

Lasco, Gideon (2022): Decolonizing harm reduction. In: Harm Reduction Journal 19, H. 8

Stöver, H./ Michels, I.I: Development of social work in prevention and treatment of HIV/AIDS and HCV in Central Asia. In: Drugs, Habits and Social Policy (in press)

Table of Contents

PART I

1. History of drug treatment services in Central Asia and China   11

1.1. *Kazakhstan: Social work and strengthening NGOs in development cooperation for drug addiction treatment in Kazakhstan*   11
Nurlan Baigabyl

1.2. *Kyrgyzstan: History of drug addiction and treatment in Kyrgyzstan*   32
Jarkyn Shadymanova and Nurgul Musaeva

1.3. *Uzbekistan: History of drug addiction and treatment in Uzbekistan*   46
Akhatjon Nasullaev

1.4. *China: History of development of addiction treatment social work in China*   53
Hang Su

PART II

Developments in the medication-assisted treatment for opioid users in Central Asia and China: Barriers and facilitators   73
Ingo Ilja Michels and Heino Stöver

PART III

Developments in the Role of Social Work in the treatment of drug addicted people in Central Asia and China   101
Ingo Ilja Michels et al.

Authors   139

1. History of drug treatment services in Central Asia and China

1.1. *Kazakhstan: Social work and strengthening NGOs in development cooperation for drug addiction treatment in Kazakhstan*

Nurlan Baigabyl

In Kazakhstan, social work as a public institution arose with the acquisition of independence in the mid-90s of the twentieth century. The institutionalization of social work in the Republic of Kazakhstan was carried out in difficult conditions of transition. In a short historical period, Soviet social support mechanisms were transformed into social work technologies aimed at meeting the needs of the poor and vulnerable segments of the population. However, paternalistic approaches and the predominance of the role of the state remained in the provision of special social services.

Based on international experience, the following transformational initiatives have been introduced:

- 2001 – continuous preparation of social workers in the system of higher and postgraduate education is carried out in universities.
- 2002 – in the education sector, social work was introduced by the Law "On social and medical and pedagogical correctional support for children with disabilities" (Law, 2002), which in 2005 was transferred to the social protection system.
- 2004 – was created the Association of Social Workers of Kazakhstan, bringing together the academic community, the practical "field" of experts in the development of educational standards in the specialties "social work" of the bachelor's and master's programs.
- 2008 – The Law on Special Social Services (Parliament of the Republic of Kazakhstan, 2008) introduces broader responsibilities of various sectors for the provision of special social services, which contributes to an increase in the number of social workers and social work specialists. This normative act at one time gave a special impetus to a unique stage in the formation and formation of social work as a profession in Kazakhstan.

- 2010 – social work was introduced in the health sector to strengthen preventive work at the PHC level (in polyclinics). The MoH introduced a case management system and a mechanism to support interdisciplinary work (Yessimova et al., 2021).
- 2017 – at the First Forum of Social Workers of Kazakhstan, the Concept for further modernization of the social service system was presented, which paid special attention to the tasks of staffing the transformation of the social service system, which will improve the quality of social services and expand the availability of social services. But this concept was left without proper state support.
- 2018 – In social protection, when reforming the system of targeted social assistance, social work consultants appear at the district level in the departments of employment and social programs. In the same year, the Project Office "National Resource Center for Social Work" was opened under the Ministry of Labor and Social Protection; According to experts, the current situation did not allow reforming the existing social work in the country and the residual principle of financing remained, which in 2021 led to the closure of the Project Office.
- 2019 – was created a public organization National Alliance of Professional Social Workers of Kazakhstan, which was supposed to replace the Resource Center and develop a new concept for the development of social work.
- In 2020, within the framework of the project (UN UNICEF, coordinator Baigabylov N.O.), an analysis of educational programs (hereinafter referred to as EP) was carried out for compliance with the descriptors of 9 international competencies of a social worker (CSWE, 2015) among the universities of Kazakhstan involved in the preparation of bachelors of Social Work in accordance with the table of registers of educational programs.

According to the Ministry of Education and Science of the Republic of Kazakhstan, there are 128 universities in the country as a whole, of which 57 are private universities (47.5 %); 22 (18.33 %) joint-stock universities; 29 (24.17 %) state universities; 1 (0.83 %) an international university and 11 (9.17 %) national higher education institutions. The number of all institutions is 120; of which are 95 (76.17 %) universities; 17 (14.17 %) academies; and 8 (6.67 %) institutes (ESUVO, 2021)

On the website of the Unified Management System for Higher Education (ESUVO, 2021), Educational Programs (EP) for all 14 universities preparing bachelors in the specialty "Social work" are available in the public domain:

The types and content of the above 9 international competencies of a social worker were the basic working units for the analysis of educational programs (EP). Based on the analysis of educational programs (EP), the following conclusions can be drawn:

- there is a problem of inconsistency between learning outcomes and types (content) of disciplines;
- in general, the learning outcomes in the EP do not fully reveal the role of a social worker to the extent that it is modeled in the criteria of international competencies of a social worker;
- assessment and intervention skills, ethical skills of a social worker in the learning outcomes of the EP are generally not reflected, since they are required and formulated in the international competencies of a social worker.

Taking into account the results of the analysis of the EP, it is recommended that all universities revise the formed learning outcomes in the EP in Social Work in accordance with the international competencies of a social worker, and include the relevant academic disciplines in the mandatory component of the EP.

In 2019, NCE RK "Atameken"[1] developed the sectoral qualifications framework "Social security and social services" (atameken.kz, 2021) in accordance with Article 117 of the Labor Code of the Republic of Kazakhstan dated November 23, 2015 and Methodological recommendations for the development and execution of sectoral qualifications frameworks, approved by the order of the Minister of Labor and Social Protection of the Population of the Republic of Kazakhstan dated January 18, 2019, No. 25.

The general position of the sectoral qualification framework included the concepts of "social worker", "social work", "supervision", "case management", "difficult life situation", "intervention". There are 42 normative legal acts regulating social relations and social work.

An analysis of the current state of social security and social services in Kazakhstan shows that there is an increase in social assistance and services provided by the state, but in parallel there is a decrease in the recipients of this support. Accordingly, new approaches to the social security system

---

1 The non-governmental organization "National Chamber of Entrepreneurs" Atameken ", which develops professional standards for all professions in Kazakhstan, in the article we wanted to indicate that we have developed college-level social work professions. Directions of case management, supervision, needs assessment are not currently available.

and to the qualification requirements of specialists are required. Thus, in 2019, a project was launched to introduce an integrated model for the provision of special social services, which is being piloted in 11 regions of the country.

Today, professional standards have been developed and approved by the Order of the Deputy Chairman of the Board of NCE RK "Atameken" dated December 18, 2019 No. 255 in accordance with the industry quali-fication framework "Special social services provided by organizations of a stationary type", "Social services for persons with hearing disabilities", "Social services for people with visual impairments" (atameken.kz, 2021).

Within the framework of these professional standards, there are no specialists of the 6th level (Activity requiring the synthesis of special [theoretical and practical] knowledge [including innovative] and practical experience [independent research, analysis and evaluation of professional information]).

An analysis of the functional duties, professional roles and qualification requirements for social workers shows that the requirements are very low, primarily due to the fact that social workers perform standard and simple similar practical tasks and they need to receive professional education with the introduction of ethical clearance. and aptitude, advanced training and certification systems with alternative forms of education.

In the system of social protection, several national projects are currently operating, which are aimed at building an integrated model of social services and social assistance. For example, "benefit plus", "integrated social services", "progressive-universal model in Primary Health Care (in polyclinics)".

The peculiarity of social work with drug addicts is that, as a professional activity, it is formed at the junction of two independent ministries – healthcare and social protection of the population. Domestic and foreign experience shows that, despite the ongoing coordination of efforts to help people with both medical and social problems, the actual coordination of departmental actions is not effective enough.

Another priority problem is the development of medical and social work in narcology, taking into account the peculiarities of the organiza-tion of the healthcare system and social protection, as well as taking into account the specifics of the socio-economic situation in Kazakhstan.

Optimal interaction is developed only after long-term joint work in the related sector, after appropriate preparation and selection of special forms of work that allow to combine the actions of representatives of different specialties in the person of a new social work specialist who has received the appropriate medical (in our case, narcological) specialization.

In practice, medical workers are forced to perform a number of functions of social workers – domestic graduates in social work have appeared only in recent years and their number is insignificant. In turn, social workers in their work very often work with clients who suffer from physical pathology.

To show the place of medical and social work among related activities, it is necessary to note the coordinating role of a social worker in resolving the whole range of problems of a client who finds himself in a difficult life situation and requires the participation of specialists in related professions – medical doctors, psychologists, teachers, and other specialists.

The model of organizing social work, including in the field of drug treatment, is the most progressive and effective; but it needs to be taken into account and mastered in the process of training social workers in Kazakhstan. Thus, the areas of activity of a social work specialist in any area of social assistance stem from his main functions of diagnostic, prognostic, human rights, organizational, preventive, socio-medical.

An increasing number of programs for the rehabilitation of persons dependent on PAS (psychoactive substances) are being developed and implemented in practice with the direct participation of social work specialists, therefore, the activity of a social work specialist in a drug treatment facility is becoming increasingly important.

The activities of a social work specialist at the medical and social stage of helping drug addicts are as follows:

- solving organizational and therapeutic problems in close cooperation with medical personnel;
- organization and participation in special psychological trainings that promote early readaptation and rehabilitation of patients;
- organization of family psychotherapy and participation in it;
- organization and participation in various programs of rehabilitation and readaptation of patients.

The functions of social work specialists dealing with problems of drug addiction, and the amount of knowledge they need for effective work, are determined by the job responsibilities of a social worker.

A social work specialist determines the system of socio-psychological and socio-legal relations in the field of prevention and treatment of drug addiction.

In the field of rehabilitation: coordinates the rehabilitation of the client in the family, helps in solving social problems, cooperating with state, public and private organizations.

With the introduction of the new law, the qualification requirements for social workers in the field of social protection of the population and healthcare (MLSP RK, 2018) were approved, which determined the necessary amount of knowledge, skills and abilities for the work performed, taking into account the level of education, new positions appeared in the social service sector: specialist in needs assessment and identification, social work specialist, social work assistant, etc. This made it possible for the social service sector to expand the staffing and reduce the number of medical positions by 31.2 %, the number of which has always been predominant in social services due to the presence of a medical model of care. As a result, the number of positions involved in the direct provision of special social services increased by 66 %, or from 21 to 35 positions.

Today, more than 15 thousand social workers work in the system of social protection and healthcare, including social care workers (72.9 % of all positions of social workers). According to the data for 2018, more than 10 thousand people work in the system of social protection of the population, more than 90 % are women. The average salary of social workers in 2021 is on average 150,000 tenge ($357) (312 €). According to a study in Zhambyl, Akmola and Pavlodar regions, 64.8 % of social workers have a higher humanitarian education.

One of the priority directions of the state social policy of Kazakhstan is the development of social assistance to the population in a difficult life situation, and sometimes in a crisis situation. These vulnerable populations include people living with HIV (PLHIV), including HIV-positive injecting drug users.

The tasks of combating HIV / AIDS and other infectious diseases formed the basis of the State Health Development Program of the Republic of Kazakhstan "Salamatty Kazakhstan" for 2011–2015, the Strategy "Kazakhstan – 2050", the Plan of the Nation "100 concrete steps to implement five institutional reforms", Five social initiatives of the Head of State and the Program "Rukhani Zhangyru". The efforts made by the state made it possible to contain the HIV epidemic in the country at a concentrated stage, reduce the number of detected cases of HIV infection among people who inject drugs (PWID), reduce the frequency of HIV transmission from mother to child, and ensure all children born with HIV infection, infected mothers receive adapted milk formula free of charge, provide PLHIV with essential antiretroviral therapy (ART), and increase counseling and testing coverage (KNCDIZ, 2019).

The system of social work with people who use drugs is fragmented, sectoral and, as a rule, works in isolation, while the Ministries of Health,

Education and Social Protection of Kazakhstan develop sectoral standards for special social services, qualification requirements for social workers.

Service and care processes for people who use drugs remain vague and unclear, lacking established algorithms for the provision of special services and a clear continuity of support. The case management approach is not used as the predominant approach to special social services.

In general, the social worker's social status is low and unattractive, while there is high turnover, low wages, and unequal positions in pay and other benefits within and between sectors. All this has a negative impact on attracting and retaining high-quality specialists for this work. The material and technical base of social services is underdeveloped.

Social work with people who use drugs in Kazakhstan is in its infancy, but development in this area is slow. All social work with this group of the population is formed mainly by local non-governmental organizations (NGOs), which are funded by international donors.

The "classic" triad in the system of organizing social work in the field of problems related to medicine and health care are services aimed at all types of prevention – primary, secondary and tertiary.

We are talking about work to prevent certain abnormal phenomena[2] underlying the disease, to prevent complications and negative consequences of the disease, to readapt and rehabilitate patients, provide social assistance to them and their families, etc. It is in such a complex form that social work is built in the field of health care in general and in the narcological field in particular in many foreign countries – the USA, Germany, Italy, Austria, Great Britain, etc.

The main functions of social workers here are: early detection and identification of people with drug problems; work with such persons, their families, social environment, employers; work with family members of drug addicts; direct work with patients (in the clinical sense) with narcological diseases, their families and social environment. Less attention is paid to primary prevention work in relation to drug use – these tasks are usually assigned to educators, law enforcement officers, members of public organizations.

Compulsory drug addiction treatment is practiced in Kazakhstan. But this is possible only by a court order. Otherwise, it will be a violent deprivation of a person's freedom. Article 91 of the Criminal Code of

---

2 Prevention of the consequences of irreversible mental processes of the individual. (prevention of irreversible pathologies in the human psyche)

the Republic of Kazakhstan spells out the grounds for the application of compulsory medical measures. They apply to people:

- Having committed the acts provided for by the articles of the Special Part of this Code, in a state of insanity.
- Who, after the commission of a criminal offense, has developed a mental disorder that makes it impossible to assign or carry out punishment.
- Committed a criminal offense and suffering from mental disorders that do not exclude sanity.
- Having committed a criminal offense and found to be in need of treatment for alcoholism, drug addiction or substance abuse.

Drug dispensaries in Kazakhstan use three main methods of treatment and treatment protocols are the same throughout the country.

Ambulatory (outpatient) treatment. A person is hospitalized in an acute condition. After the abrupt cessation of drug use, a withdrawal syndrome occurs. Doctors are struggling with withdrawal symptoms. The first step is to detoxify the body. For this, various means are used: from a dropper to special liquid solutions that relieve intoxication in the body.

Medical treatment. It can be carried out on an outpatient basis: the patient is prescribed special drugs, these are often antipsychotics, various adsorbents and nootropics. However, doctors note that there is no specific cure for drug addiction and treatment is purely individual.

Rehabilitation. The most important stage of treatment. After the organism is cleansed of poisons, the physically ill person feels better. But he falls out of his usual way of life, and he has not yet formed a new one. Therefore, psychological help is important at this stage.

In drug dispensaries, addicts are treated free of charge. But there are also paid programs. In this case, the patient is anonymized, the patient will not be put on a special account. In Kazakhstan, among state institutions (services are free), one clinic in the city of Pavlodar can provide complete anonymity even without a residence permit (registration at the place of residence), other centers do not provide services without registering a residence permit in their region and official registration. Anonymity is also provided by commercial clinics.

The methods of treatment in private clinics, of course, differ from those used in drug dispensaries. But they require financial investment.

A day of stay in hospitals costs 9–10 thousand tenge (23 $) (20 €) and more. It is also worth considering the cost of medicines, procedures (for example, blood purification with a laser), psychologist services, and so on. On average, treatment cost can start at 800 $ and up.

Experts identify three main causes of drug addiction: genetic predisposition, social environment, psychological cause.

International rehabilitation networks also operate in Kazakhstan. One of them, for example, is the "Renaissance" center with branches in Karaganda, Almaty and Astana. Center identifies four types of addiction treatment:

1) Medical – coding, the use of drugs that block the action of narcotic substances.
2) Stationary – six months to a year of compulsory treatment.
3) Rehabilitation – work with a psychologist, psychotherapist, possibly a psychotherapist. Also work with anonymous groups.
4) Detox – measures to cleanse the body.

"Opioid substitution therapy" (OST) (Opioid Agonist Treatment – OAT)[3]

In Kazakhstan, (in Kazakhstan with methadone only) OST has been implemented since 2008 with the support of the Global Fund to Fight AIDS, Tuberculosis and Malaria and is recommended for the treatment of drug addicted patients and the prevention of HIV-AIDS. Within 12 years (2008–2020), 1331 patients received OST treatment in 10 regions of the country.

As of December 31, 2019, there were 296 people in treatment, which is only 0.3 % of the estimated number of people who use opioid drugs (94,600) (Abishev, 2020), of which 235 were men and 61 were women. In July 2021, 326 people are participating in the program, 117 of them are HIV patients (azattyq.org, 2021). In 2019, 44 people were accepted into the program. The number of PLHIV in the program is 109, of which 92 (84 %) are taking ART (Abishev, 2020).

According to doctors, the program has shown its effectiveness. According to the Mental Health Center, 330 participants routinely completed the program with positive results; 127 participants found families; 560 people were employed. There is a decrease in the criminal behavior of program participants: 78 % (1038 participants) had criminal experience before being included in the program, of which 565 people had multiple convictions. Over 12 years of program implementation, 61 program participants were convicted (azattyq.org, 2021).

---

3 The term OST had been replaced by OAT to make it clear that it is not a "replacement" but a treatment witg agonists. Occasionally, the term Medication Assisted Treatment (MAT) is also used.

Taking into account our HIV epidemiological situation and provision of OST/OAT to less than 1 % of PLHIV/PWID, it is possible to prevent only 5 cases of HIV infection. With an increase in coverage of PLHIV/PWID with a program supporting substitution therapy up to 20 %, it will prevent up to 100 new cases of HIV infection, and 40 % coverage of OST/OAT for PLHIV/PWID will prevent up to 200 cases of HIV. Thus, the current coverage of OST/OAT for PWID does not affect the epidemic situation of HIV infection in the country (Abishev, 2020).

The outpatient drug addiction network in 2019 is represented by 209 drug treatment rooms, except for dispensaries (2014 – 187 drug treatment rooms), of which 149 rooms (2014 – 120) are located in rural areas. In the private healthcare sector of the Republic of Kazakhstan, 18 drug treatment rooms were registered in 2019 (22 in 2014) (mentalcenter.kz, 2020).

The percentage of people who inject drugs among patients with addiction to drugs and psychotropic substances in the Republic of Kazakhstan (RK) in 2019 was 61.5 % (in 2018 64.9 %, 2017–64., 9 %, 2016 – 97.2 %, 2015 – 92.2 %, 2014 – 65.9 %, 2013 – 66.7 %).

The proportion of female PWID among the group of patients with dependence on drugs and psychotropic substances, who are injecting, in 2019 was 9.5 % (in 2018 – 10.9 %, 2017 – 10.6 %, 2016 – 10.5 %, 2015 – 9.9 %, 2014 – 7.0 %, 2013 – 7.3 %), the proportion of minors – 0.2 % (in 2018 – 0.3 %, 2017 – 0.07 %, 2016 – 0.05 %, 2015 – 0.03 %, 2014 – 0.01 %, 2013 – 0.04 %) (mentalcenter.kz, 2020).

To establish the average number of methadone users under the OST/OAT program, calculations were made based on the state quota for narcotic drugs for medical consumption, approved by the Government of the Republic of Kazakhstan (adilet.zan.kz, 2021).

According to the standard (Order, 2020), the daily dose is 60–120 mg per person taking methadone under the OST program (Fig. 1). It is assumed that the estimated number of methadone users in the country for 2021 is expected to be from 700 to 1400 people. (calculation of need / (daily dose * 365 days).

The program has been implemented in a pilot mode from 2008 to the present day.

The program exists and is funded by the Global Fund (mgorod.kz, 2020). This may be evidenced by the fact that in 2021 a grant agreement for 2021–2023 was signed between the Ministry of Health of Kazakhstan and the Global Fund (azattyq.org, 2021).

Of the drugs that have been used in OST/OAT since 2015, methadone has been registered in Kazakhstan under the code RK-LS-No121922 and is approved for use (mk-kz.kz, 2019).

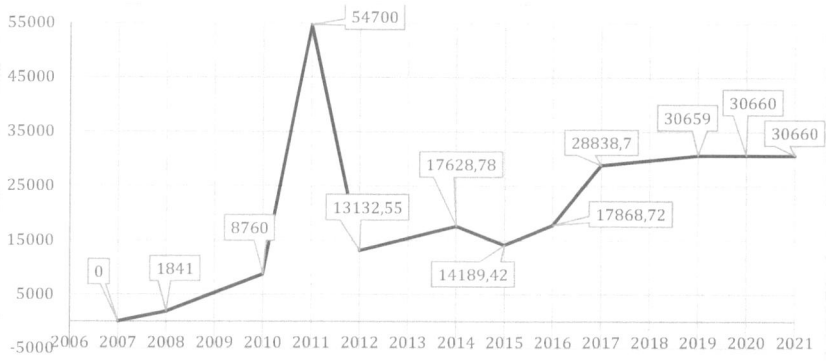

Picture 1: Quota of methadone in the Republic of Kazakhstan for legal entities, for medical purposes[4]

OST/OAT is a method of long-term (more than six months) care using drugs classified as opiate agonists, in combination with the provision of psychosocial care for people suffering from opioid dependence (Mentalcenter, 2015).

The price of methadone, about 1 USD (informburo.kz, 2017), is low.

Medical and social assistance and services for people participating in OST/OAT are provided by opioid agonist maintenance therapy rooms. In the offices according to the standard (Order, 2020) provides the following services:

- services under the program of maintenance therapy with opioid agonists, including the issuance of drugs, psychosocial counseling in accordance with the approved clinical protocol;
- improving the quality of life and social adaptation of patients with opioid dependence;
- reducing the frequency and volume of the use of illegal narcotic drugs and psychotropic substances;
- reducing the risk of transmission of HIV infection and other comorbidities among injecting drug users;
- increasing adherence to antiretroviral therapy of persons infected with HIV infection, dependent on opioids.

---

4 Quantity (limit) of methadone (official unit of measurement in grams), which is allowed to be imported into Kazakhstan. For example, for 2021 the quota is 30660 grams.

Indications for the appointment of maintenance therapy with opioid agonists are the presence of all the main and one of the additional criteria. Main criteria: diagnosis "Opioid addiction (F11.2)"; ability to give informed consent; age over 18 years old. Additional criteria: established diagnosis of HIV infection; established diagnosis of hepatitis B, C, D, G; proven experience of injecting drug use for at least 3 years; at least two hospitalizations in a hospital with a diagnosis of "Opioid addiction (F11.2)"; pregnancy.

OST/OAT therapy rooms operate in 15 cities: Almaty, Uralsk, Atyrau, Aktobe, Semey, Ust-Kamenogorsk, Pavlodar, Ekibastuz, Karaganda, Temirtau, Taraz, Kostanay, Rudny, Lisakovsk and Kyzylorda. Further expansion of the program is being considered (azattyq.org, 2021). Time of issuing and receiving methadone daily from 8.00 am to 10.00 am (mgorod.kz, 2020).

The initial daily dose of methadone hydrochloride is determined by the level of neuroadaptation to opioids with tolerance to opiates, an initial dose of 10 mg is indicated, and with an established physical dependence, the initial dose is 20–30 mg. The duration of the patient's stay at this stage is 6 months or more. The optimal dose of methadone hydrochloride is 60–120 mg per day. In case of planned completion/early withdrawal of treatment, the daily dose of the drug can be reduced by an average of 2.5 – 5 mg per week, without severe symptoms of opioid withdrawal. During the decline, the patient should be regularly examined, and according to clinical need, adjustments in dosages should be made. In case of exclusion of the patient, it is recommended to reduce the dose of the drug by 5 mg daily until reaching 30 mg. Further, the daily dose reduction of the drug should be 2 mg until complete withdrawal.

In all these cases, the possibility of developing a dose reduction scheme for the drug by the attending physician together with the patient individually is not excluded. In patients diagnosed with TB, the initial priority of the service is to treat active tuberculosis (TB), i.e. while they are in hospital, methadone is not available to them. For patients with viral hepatitis, treatment is carried out in combination with other pharmacotherapy, without waiting for the onset of opioid withdrawal. HIV patients are first stabilized with OST/OAT, followed by antiretroviral therapy. In pregnancy and breastfeeding, opioid agonist maintenance treatment with methadone is the most appropriate treatment (Mentalcenter, 2015).

Psychosocial support for OST/OAT patients includes motivational interviewing and cognitive behavioral therapy (Mentalcenter, 2015).

The number of patients receiving methadone is only about 2 % of all injecting drug users registered at the dispensary. This low number of drug addicts on methadone therapy is due to the stringent requirements. The procedure looks like this: volunteers come daily to the drug dispensary, where, under the supervision of medical staff, they receive their "narcotic ration". Methadone is not issued "on hand" (in case of hospitalization for other diseases, rehabilitation in centers located in other cities, travel on a business trip and if patients end up in prison, methadone is not issued, a mandatory requirement to come to the office for providing maintenance therapy with opioid agonists at the Centers mental health). In Kazakhstan, the condition is mandatory in the contract – not to use other drugs. Participants in the program are checked every week. These surveys, by the way, are also expensive. However, many are not ready to fulfill so many conventions for the sake of a "free dose". Hence the small number of participants (mk-kz.kz, 2019).

According to narcologists, methadone therapy does not cure drug addiction by 100 %. At the same time, it makes life easier for patients – to return them to society, control the risks of contracting incurable diseases and significantly reduce the level of crime (mk-kz.kz, 2019).

Patients who are on OST/OAT have positive results. Two expert assessments on the implementation of therapy (the last one was carried out by international experts from Columbia University in 2012) confirmed this: many patients found a family, a job, stopped thinking about searching for drugs, and, in general, returned to society. Some of them have completely abandoned drug use and are now helping others (mk-kz.kz, 2019).

The project was checked in 2010 by the Ministry of Health, then on behalf of the Security Council of Kazakhstan in 2015 by the Prosecutor General's Office. Then it was recommended to terminate it ahead of schedule and withdraw patients from the program with a gradual reduction in the dose of methadone. The Prosecutor General's Office considered it inappropriate to continue OST/OAT. In the monograph "Formation and development prospects of the institute for assessing the level of drug use in Kazakhstan" – a study by researchers from the Academy of Law Enforcement Agencies under the Prosecutor General's Office, the following reasons are noted:

- failed to reduce the incidence of HIV infection; the project does not provide for the resocialization of persons undergoing treatment;
- lack of motivation to give up drugs;
- pronounced aggressive behavior during methadone withdrawal ("withdrawal");
- lack of effect of education of law-abiding behavior.

It also says that by the protocol decision of the meeting of the IMS (interdepartmental headquarters for coordinating the activities of state bodies aimed at combating drug addiction and drug trafficking) in 2018, "a recommendation was given to the Ministry of Health on the inappropriateness of using OST/OAT" (azattyq.org, 2021)

In June 2017, the Ministry of Internal Affairs of the Republic of Kazakhstan demanded to stop the implementation of the program, after which they created an Intersectoral Working Group of 17 people, whose task was to evaluate its effectiveness. The working group prepared a resolution concluding that OST/OAT is effective in Kazakhstan and should be continued, but some of its members initiated an alternative study with the assistance of the police. The conclusions of the alternative examination turned out to be predictable, so in January 2018, the admission of new patients in the opioid substitution therapy centers was temporarily stopped. Meanwhile, the Kazakhstan Union of HIV-infected people appealed to the President of the country not to close the project (mk-kz.kz, 2019).

Parliamentarians have also repeatedly spoken out against the implementation of the opioid substitution therapy program in Kazakhstan (zakon.kz, 2014). In particular, deputies from the Ak Zhol party (akzhol.kz, 2017) believe that an analogue of heroin and morphine can undermine national security in the country. In support of this, the following fact was cited: in the document "Expanding the availability of opioid substitution therapy in the Republic of Kazakhstan in 2010–2014: an overview of the situation, an action plan and an operational implementation plan", it was noted that a delay in the supply of methadone for at least one day threatens the country with socio-political unrest (mk-kz.kz, 2019).

Arguments against opioid agonist maintenance therapy:

- "Harm reduction programs", including OST/OAT, are imposed on us by the West and are carried out for the most part with Western money coming from abroad through non-governmental organizations (Ieromonakh, Shevtsova, & Kaklyugin, 2007), under the guise of this program, a new type of drug business (mk-kz.kz, 2019);
- studies and clinical trials of methadone in Kazakhstan were conducted in violation of legal requirements and in favor of OST/OAT (mk-kz.kz, 2019) (Ieromonakh, Shevtsova, & Kaklyugin, 2007) (In 2011, after the results of the pilot project, a negative the conclusion of an independent commission, but for unknown reasons, the results of this check are hushed up (zakon.kz, nd));

- within the framework of the program, it has not yet been possible to achieve the goal – the complete resocialization of drug addicts (mk-kz.kz, 2019);
- the methadone program can lead to mass riots (akzhol.kz, 2017) (This was confirmed by the fact that the supply of methadone in Temirtau failed, when, due to the lack of another drug ration, patients began to experience a pronounced picture of "withdrawal" with manifestations of aggression, depression, pain manifestations, disruption of relationships in the family. (zakon.kz, n.d.));
- the use of "Methadone" is not a treatment for a drug addict, but only serves to transfer him to a harder drug with more detrimental consequences. (akzhol.kz, 2017).

Non-Governmental organizations (NGOs)

More than 1,500 non-governmental organizations (NGOs) that receive state funding are registered on the official websites of the NJSC "Center for Support of Civil Initiatives" and public procurement of the Republic of Kazakhstan.

Analysis of the official website of the NJSC "Center for Support of Civic Initiatives" reprt that more than 200 NGOs are registered (cisc.kz, 2021). The mission of the NAO "Center for Support of Civic Initiatives" is to assist NGOs in the implementation of social projects of the state.

According to the NJSC "Center for Support of Civil Initiatives" for 2017–2021. a total of 308 projects, of which 84 (27.3 %) are aimed at promoting the development of civil society, 55 (17.8 %) – supporting youth policy and children's initiatives, 54 (17.5 %) – protecting the rights and legitimate interests of citizens and organizations, 16 (5.2 %) – achieving goals in the field of education, science, information, physical culture and sports, 8 (2.5 %) – health protection and promotion of a healthy lifestyle (cisc.kz, 2021). There are no state/budget funding projects for social support for PWID people, in 2021 three projects were implemented from a donor organization National Institute on Drug Abuse Problems (USA) (сайт https://infonpo.gov.kz/web/guest/otkrytyj-reestr-proektov-npo).

Despite discussions in society and government offices, in 2019 the Ministry of Health adopted an Order approving the Roadmap for the implementation of the maintenance substitution therapy program for people suffering from opioid dependence in the Republic of Kazakhstan for 2019–2020 (Order (1), 2019).

However, along with the adoption of an official document that seemed to stimulate the spread of this therapy, patients faced some problems. During the meeting of the working groups of the Country Coordinating Committee on work with international organizations on HIV infection and tuberculosis with NGOs, which was held in Almaty in May 2021, it was reported that patients with HIV status will now be able to receive substitution therapy until the end of the year. As representatives of the Republican Scientific and Practical Center for Mental Health noted, the amount of methadone is limited, enough for 700 patients. By the end of the year, the department plans to develop a schedule, for all methadone dispensing points, new and existing, there are quotas for the recruitment of 450 HIV-infected patients (oskementv.kz, 2019).

According to official data from the Ministry of Health, in 2020, 20,259 Kazakhstanis were registered with drug addiction, which is 107 people per 100,000 population, the ratio of women to men was 1:11. The age of consumers is most often 35–45 years.

In 2020, out of 20,000 registered patients, 3,266 patients received inpatient treatment at public mental health centers.

Medical and Social Rehabilitation

A comprehensive program of medical and social rehabilitation for patients with dependence on psychoactive substances (PS) is carried out within the framework of the guaranteed volume of free medical care (GOBMP). In 2021, more than 37 million tenge (86.6 thousand $)(76 thousand €) were allocated for the treatment of patients with drug addiction to all mental health centers across the country. This amount includes not only inpatient but also outpatient treatment, as well as the work of the mental health service.

This is dynamic: monitoring, anti-relapse therapy, prevention, medical examinations, temporary detoxification and adaptation centers, prevention of suicidal behavior, this are completely all parts of inpatient treatment.

Hospitalization can take over a year. At the first stage of the so-called withdrawal, the patient is hospitalized and prescribed medication.

At the second stage, intensive psychotherapy is connected, which can last up to four months. After that, the patient has the opportunity to stay in the department of social rehabilitation, where he will spend another nine months. People who underwent inpatient treatment in Kazakhstan continue to be registered with drug addiction.

After the patient completes the rehabilitation program, a period of abstinence of a year or more is monitored. When patients arrive, they sign an agreement that in a year they will be asked about their future fate. And they leave contacts for communication – their own and relatives.

Kazakhstan does not have separate hotlines for drug addicts. Officially, in the system of psychiatric services, helplines are more directed towards people with a high suicidal risk.

There is a website that does not require any identification, where anyone who needs it can apply absolutely free and anonymously, and receive free psychological help (https://www.na-kz.com/).

Peer-to-peer-education

Since 2007, the "School of Volunteers" has been operating at the RSPC MSPS, the main task of which is to train former injecting drug users to work in harm reduction programs based on the "Peer to Peer" principle.

A study of a number of international standards in the field of case management suggests the following: case management is the main approach through which drug users can access medical, legal and other services.

The Accompanying Specialist, which may be a social worker, acts as an intermediary and represents the drug addict in help services. In the process of informing and educating the addict in the use of available resources, the escort assesses the addict's needs and monitors the progress of the situation. The Accompanying Specialist identifies and works with the needs of the addict in terms of physical and psychosocial well-being, education, management of their own risk factors for drug dependence, and issues related to access to health services and support: drug dependence treatment, counseling, legal assistance and assistance in finding employment, etc.

Of particular interest in this regard are the recommendations of experts from the United Nations Office on Drugs and Crime, which took into account the positive experience gained in the field of social support. These recommendations are freely available at: https://www.unodc.org/document s/russia/Manuals/case_management_guidelines_UNODC.pdf

Advanced training program for social workers and employees performing social work functions

The definition of a social worker and the requirements for the preparation of a number of new standards in this area, including those aimed at improving and ensuring the quality of the profession, are contained in the Law of the Republic of Kazakhstan dated December 29, 2008 No. 114-IV "On Special Social Services" (hereinafter – SSS).

However, although the legislation defines social work and social workers, these definitions are not standardized across sectors, nor are they fully consistent with international definitions and the concept of the profession. For example, the definition in the SSS Law[5]limits the profession to two functions (providing SSS and/or conducting needs assessments) and misses the broader concept underlying the key principles of social work. The definition also emphasizes the current approach to SSS as being reactive, reacting when a problem occurs, rather than focusing on prevention and early detection and intervention of social and other risks.

Qualification provisions are weak and vaguely define the various (all) social welfare professions, their roles and responsibilities, including care processes, competency levels and qualifications. There is no single registration and certification system for social workers and no body to oversee this core component of quality assurance. While social workers in health and social care are required to undergo a proficiency test every five years, these procedures do not appear to be standardized across the country, including lack of clear provisions regarding examination requirements. Codes of conduct are not established, limited opportunities exists to enhance individual accountability of social workers, e.g. through an established complaints mechanism, strong oversight, mentorship and support mechanisms, clearly established and appropriate performance indicators for social workers and other professionals performing these functions.

Thus, a unified advanced training program for social workers and employees performing the functions of social work is not approved by the legislation of Kazakhstan.

---

5 In Kazakhstan, the functions of a social worker are enshrined in the law "On Special Social Services (SSU)", the name of special social services is due to the fact that services are provided not for everyone, but for citizens who find themselves in a difficult life situation.

Guidelines for developing local terminology and concepts

When developing local terminology and concepts, you can be guided by the following current regulations:

- Law of the Republic of Kazakhstan dated July 10, 1998 N 279 "On narcotic drugs, psychotropic substances, their analogues and precursors and measures to counter their illicit trafficking and abuse";
- Code of the Republic of Kazakhstan dated July 7, 2020 N360-VI LRK "On the health of the people and the healthcare system";
- Documents of the United Nations Office on Drugs and Crime (UN-ODC, 2016).

References

Abisheyev, A. T. (2020). *Issues of dermatology and Infections* (1–2), 29–36.

adilet.zan.kz. (2021). *On approval of the state quota of the Republic of Kazakhstan for narcotic drugs, psychotropic substances and precursors for 2000–2021.* Information received from ADILET: https://adilet.zan.kz/rus/search/docs/

akzhol.kz. (24 05 2017 г.). *Why is the drug "Methadone", prohibited by the UN Convention for use for medical purposes, officially used in our country as a substitution therapy drug? Retrieved from Official website of the Ak Zhol Democratic Party*: https://akzhol.kz/ru/migrated_4694/

atameken.kz. (2021). *NATIONAL QUALIFICATION SYSTEM IN THE REPUBLIC OF KAZAKHSTAN: HISTORY, DEVELOPMENT, RESULTS. Received from the National Chamber of Entrepreneurs of the Republic of Kazakhstan "Atameken"*: https://atameken.kz/ru/services/16

azattyq.org. (15 07 2021 г.). Derived from Methadone: Evil or Good? What will happen to substitution therapy for drug addicts: https://rus.azattyq.org/a/kazakhstan-methadone-drug-addiction-treatment-project/31356654.html

cisc.kz. (2021). *Projects. Received from NAO "Center for Support of Civic Initiatives"*: https://cisc.kz/projects

CSWE. (2015). *2015-EPAS.* Information received from Council on Social Work Education: https://www.cswe.org/getattachment/Accreditation/Accreditation-Process/2015-EPAS/2015EPAS_Web_FINAL.pdf.aspx

ESUVO. (2021). *Register of educational programs. Received on 12 2021, from UNIFIED MANAGEMENT SYSTEM OF HIGHER EDUCATION Ministry of Education and Science of the Republic of Kazakhstan*: http://esuvo.platonus.kz/#/register/education_program

informburo.kz. (11 06 2017 г.). Received 2021, from Free methadone dispensing point to be opened in Atyrau drug dispensary: https://informburo.kz/novosti/punkt-besplatnoy-vydachi-metadona-otkroyut-v-narkodispansere-atyrau.html

Hieromonk, A. B., Shevtsova, Yu. B., & Kaklyugin, N. V. (2007). BEWARE – METHADONE!!! Information received from http://www.blaivus.org/UserFiles/blaivi_karta/.pdf

Kazakh Scientific Center of Dermatology and Infectious disease. (2019). Country Progress Report – Kazakhstan.. Global Monitoring of the AIDS Epidemic 2019. (PhD, Compiler) Kazakhstan. Received 24 12 2020 г., http://www.kncdiz.kz/files/00007835.pdf

Law, R. K. (July 11, 2002). "On social and medical-pedagogical correctional support for children with disabilities". Received 2021, from Information and legal system of normative legal acts of the Republic of Kazakhstan: https://adilet.zan.kz/rus/docs/Z020000343_

Mentalcenter. (2015). *Mental and behavioral disorders caused by the use of opioids, maintenance opiate agonist replacement therapy. Received 2021, from RSE on REM "Republican Scientific and Practical Center for Mental Health" of the Ministry of Health of the Republic of Kazakhstan*: https://storages.medelement.com/uploads/co/92401378980547/documents/fa0dcaf2c1d2efae56d118cda703a7d1.pdf

mentalcenter.kz. (2020). *NARCOLOGICAL AID TO THE POPULATION OF THE REPUBLIC OF KAZAKHSTAN FOR 2018–2019 (Statistical compendium). Received 2021, from RSE on REM "Republican Scientific and Practical Center for Mental Health" of the Ministry of Health of the Republic of Kazakhstan*: http://mentalcenter.kz

Ministry of Finance. (2021). Received from Public Procurement of the Ministry of Finance of the Republic of Kazakhstan: https://goszakup.gov.kz/

Ministry of Labor and Social Protection of Population of the RK. (August 14, 2018). Decree of the Minister of Labor and Social Protection of the Population of the Republic of Kazakhstan "On approval of qualification requirements for social workers". Received 2021, from Information and legal system of normative legal acts of the Republic of Kazakhstan: https://adilet.zan.kz/rus/docs/V1800017383

mgorod.kz. (03 11 2020 г.). Derived from 5 years without heroin: how the life of Ural addicts has changed with methadone therapy: https://mgorod.kz/nitem/5-let-bez-geroina-kak-izmenilas-zhizn-uralskix-narkomanov-s-metadonovoj-terapiej/

mk-kz.kz. (12 07 2019 г.). «*MK in Kazakhstan*». Derived 2021, from Methadone: Evil or Good?: https://mk-kz.kz/social/2019/07/12/metadon-dlya-narkozavisimykh-blago-ili-zlo.html

Order. (2020). Order of the Minister of Health of the Republic of Kazakhstan dated November 30, 2020 On approval of the standard for organizing the provision of medical and social assistance in the field of mental health to the population of the Republic of Kazakhstan. Retrieved from https://adilet.zan.kz/rus/docs/V2000021712

Order(1). (2019). Order of the Minister of Health of the Republic of Kazakhstan dated May 8, 2019 No. 196 On approval of the Roadmap for the implementation of the maintenance substitution therapy program for people suffering from opioid addiction in the Republic of Kazakhstan for 2019–2020. Received 2021, http://pdo-zhambyl.kz/resources

oskementv.kz. (28 06 2019 г.). *Substitution Therapy Support Program. Received from Kazakhstan» RTRK*: https://oskementv.kz/ru/news/society/programma-podderzh ki-zamestitelnoi-terapii

Parliament of the Republic of Kazakhstan. (December 29, 2008). Law of the Republic of Kazakhstan "On special social services". Received 2021, from "Adilet" Information and legal system of normative legal acts of the Republic of Kazakhstan: https://adilet.zan.kz/rus/docs/Z080000114_

UNODC. (2016). *Terminology and information on narcotic drugs. Retrieved 2021, from United Nations Office on Drugs and Crime*: https://www.unodc.org/documents/sci entific/Terminology_and_Information_on_Drugs_R_3rd_Edition.pdf

Yessimova, D. G., Baigabylov;, N. O., Kudabekov, M. M., Baltabayeva, Zh. B., Mukasheva, D. D., & Zhamankuliva, Zh. S. (2021). Social work with people living with HIV infection and drug users in Kazakhstan. "Bulletin of the Eurasian National University named after L.N. Gumilyov. Series Pedagogy. Psychology. Sociology" (3(136)), 289–300. Received from https://bulpedps.enu.kz/article/arc hive/view?id=social-work-with-people-living-with-hiv-infection-and-people-using -drugs-in-kazakhstan-2

zakon.kz. (б.д.). Received from Citizens of Kazakhstan oppose the promotion of the drug "methadone" as a means for the "treatment" of drug addicts: https://online. zakon.kz/Document/?doc_id=30955906#pos=19;-12

zakon.kz. (3 11 2014 г.). *Response to the deputy request of the Prime Minister of the Republic of Kazakhstan dated October 16, 2014 No. 20–45/4577 "On the adoption of urgent measures to ban the use of the drug "Methadone" in the Republic of Kazakhstan".* Information received from zakon.kz: https://www.zakon.kz/4664969-otv et-na-deputatskijj-zapros-premer.html

1.2. Kyrgyzstan: History of drug addiction and treatment in Kyrgyzstan

Jarkyn Shadymanova and Nurgul Musaeva

Introduction

In 90-ies drugs came from Afghanistan due to their geographic location. Kyrgyzstan borders the Republic of Tajikistan, which in turn has a common border with Afghanistan. By that time Afghanistan produced over 90 % of all illicit opiates in the world. Kyrgyzstan's territory is used for drug trafficking. According to Nogoibaev (2010) heroin occupies a leading position in consumption among locals. Officially there are 9,000 drug users registered in the country. According to experts the estimated number of injecting drug users was 25,000 people (Shebardina etc, 2015), which is almost 3 times more than official numbers, and the death rate from drug use was close to 2 % of the total number of people in 2015. (Anti-drug program of the Government of the Kyrgyz Republic, 2014). In this paper we would like to cover significant events in the history of addiction and treatment in Kyrgyzstan. Also -weI would describe the drug treatment approaches in current days.

History of Addiction

Pre-Soviet

The origin of drug distribution is connected to the so-called "opium wars" in China in 1840–1860. Since Kyrgyzstan borders with China, drugs were brought to the territory of Kyrgyzstan. It was a result of the resettlement from China at the end of the 19th century to Turkestan and Kyrgyzstan was part of the Turkestan region. The resettlement process involved Uighurs and Dungans. Among those migrants were not only smokers of opium, but also those who engaged with drug production and trade. As for the Kyrgyz and Kazakhs, due to the nomadic way of life, they did not cultivate until the end of the 19th century. Local people did not grow opium poppy, although, on the territory of Kyrgyzstan, there were lands where crops of this crop yielded high yields (Issyk-Kul region) and on which, later, under Soviet rule, they began to grow poppies for the needs of medicine. However in Turkestan, among the nomadic and sedentary population during this period, another drug of natural origin was widely distributed (Nogoibaev, 2014, 42) – a product of wild-growing hemp, called hashish and containing narcotic substances cannabinoids.

Since local people practiced a nomadic lifestyle they did not engage in cultivating opium poppy but refugees from China had experience on agriculture mainly they cultivated and smuggled to China until the emergence of the Soviet Union. As a policy of the Soviet government, local people were forced to settle down and introduced agriculture activities. Since the climate was very friendly for growing opium poppies, the government decided to cultivate this culture for medical purposes. Despite the fact that this agriculture sector was under the strict control however mass production of opium poppies caused drug addiction among local people. [Anti-drug program of the Government of the Kyrgyz Republic].

Early Soviet Time

During the soviet period, a state monopoly on the production of opium was declared in Kyrgyzstan, and the active cultivation of opium poppy for medical purposes began. This was accompanied by increased state control over its sowing and processing, which were concentrated in certain farms, later united into collective farms and state farms. There is evidence that until 1974, legally grown opium poppy was industrially processed to obtain raw opium, which accounted for about 80 % of all opium produced in the USSR and 16 % of the world's legal production of this drug. At the same time, one tenth of the produced opium went into illegal circulation, causing the population to become "drugged" [Anti-drug program of the government of the Kyrgyz Republic, www]. Hashish and marijuana were produced from wild-growing hemp (cannabis) in volumes sufficient for domestic consumption and export to other regions of the USSR. Central Asia (1924), the land allotted for opium poppy cultivation turned out to be entirely within the territory of the Kara-Kyrgyz Autonomous Region (current Kyrgyz Republic), which was part of the RSFSR. In the same year from abroad, according to the reports of JSCCPO (Joint Stock Company for the Collection and Processing of Opium) 13,980 kilograms were imported (Kurmanov, 1989). And in 1926, the country refused to import, since the need for opium for medical purposes was already completely satisfied by its own production (Isakov, 2001).

In the early years of soviet power, drug speculation was officially recognized as "the most disgusting of all kinds of speculation" and by a special order of the Council of People's Commissioners on July 31, 1918 was declared "on the fight against speculation of cocaine" the CHEKA and the police was charged with the duty "to ruthlessly arrest all these bastards who make money on complete disorder of the life and health of a huge number of people". At the same time, the criminal code of 1922 still was lacked articles providing for liability for illegal drug dealing. Such addition to the Criminal Code of USSR was made only 3 years later. According to the article 140-d, "the manufacture, possession and sale of drugs were punished with imprisonment for up to 3 years". Later adoption of the criminal code, which was adopted on November 22, 1926, already there, had norms of social protection in the form of compulsory treatment of drug addicts[1].

Further streamlining of state control over drug trafficking was the decree of the All-Central executive committee and council of people's commissars of the USSR of May 23, 1928 "on measures to regulate the trade of narcotic substances". Article 1 of the said, "decree prohibited free circulation within the country of cocaine, its salts, hashish, opium, morphine, heroin, cocaine, etc."[2] After the national-state delimitation of drugs, state policy changed and was carried out more strictly.

Soviet Period

Until 1929, i.e. prior to the beginning of the "complete collectivization" of agriculture, the protection of legal opium poppy plantations was carried out by departmental guards of the joint-stock company JSCCPO. In order to intensify the fight against drunkenness, increase the responsibility of the police for this matter, by the decision of the government of the USSR in 1939. Medical sobering-up stations are transferred from the People's Commissariat of Health to the NKVD system and are structurally included in the militia.

Throughout the years of soviet power, with the possible exception of the period of glasnost, official propaganda claimed that there was no social environment in the USSR in which drug addiction could develop. They said that "this phenomenon is characteristic exclusively of bourgeois society

---

1 On measures to regulate the trade in narcotic drugs, Decree of the Council of People's Commissars of the USSR, Decree of the Central Executive Committee of the USSR, SZ USSR, 1928, N 33, item 290.
2 ibid.

and for a long time mainly rich foreign loafers suffer from drug addiction" (Zelichenko, 2004).

The problems of drug addictions were usually solved by sending them to jail. Many of them ended up in correctional institutions when they committed crimes, trying to get money for the next dose. Drug addiction began to spread more and more widely in the criminal environment. Corrective labor colony was operating and controlled under the Inferior Affairs.

By order of the ministry of health of the USSR n143 dated 6/iv-1957, the attention of health authorities was drawn to the need to strengthen the treatment and preventive work to combat drug addiction and a special system was introduced to record people with a diagnosis of drug addiction for the first time in their lives. Also the Order N406 of the USSR Ministry of Health of November 10, 1957 established a special procedure for dispensing medicines containing narcotic substances from pharmacies (Zhirnov, 2013).

However, according to many testimonies, despite the special order, drugs continued to be bought and sold almost freely. Moreover, a surge in their consumption began shortly after the Central Committee of the CPSU and the Council of Ministers of the USSR in 1958 adopted a resolution "On intensifying the fight against drunkenness and restoring order in the trade in strong alcoholic beverages". In addition to the usual words for such documents that drunkenness is a relic of the past landowner-bourgeois system and the old way of life, and that drunkenness creates an unhealthy situation in collectives and pushes individual *irresponsible comrades* to crime, the resolution contained a lot of new things (Zhirnov, 2013). So, every drunkard, regardless of the degree of harm he caused, was ordered to be judged by a *comrades' court* in a team. And apply even more severe measures to drinking communists, up to exclusion from the party.

Later on the legislation of the RSFSR does not provide any coercive measures, except for moral ones. This circumstance complicates the actual conduct of the fight against drug addicts. So the law did not work. After all, its publication would show the country and the world that all talk about a special social environment in the USSR is complete nonsense. Citizens, without waiting for help, stopped writing about drugs, and the problem, as it were, ceased to exist by itself, although it continued to grow (Zhirnov, 2013).

In 1962, the number of detained citizens in a state of intoxication reached 37 thousand people (Plotkin, 2015). Police analysis of the state of crime showed that up to 80 % of all crimes in the republic, and for some types 100 %, committed on the basis of drunkenness. Taking into account the high degree of influence of drunkenness on the level of crime, the Ministry of Public Order of the Republic decided to convert one corrective labor colony into a medical labor dispensary (MLD) for the rehabilitation of alcoholics and drug addicts. (Plotkin, 2015).

It was said that Kyrgyz SSR legal industrial production of opium poppy supplied 80 % of all opium demand in the USSR which was 16 % of the world legal production. However, in 1974, the Presidium of the Supreme Council Soviet Union, on the base of UN recommendation, decided to end the legal cultivation of the opium poppy in the territory of Kyrgyz SSR (Nogoibaev, 2014).

In May 1985, the Central Committee of the CPSU adopted a resolution "On measures to overcome drunkenness and alcoholism", the Council of Ministers of the USSR issued a resolution "On measures to overcome drunkenness, alcoholism, the eradication of moonshine." In the course of the implementation of these resolutions, the number of outlets in the re-public selling alcoholic beverages was reduced by five times, and the sale of alcohol in 1985 was reduced by 50 % decreased by more than 20 % (Zhirnov, 2013). At the same time, a sharp restriction on the sale of alcohol gave a powerful impetus to the spread of home brewing and speculation in alcohol, contributing to the unprecedented enrichment of those involved in this criminal trade. Sugar disappeared from sale, so a rationing system had to be introduced; as consequences the drug addiction and substance abuse began to flourish. The Government plan did not worked and increased other problems with drug addiction.

Independency

If before the collapse of the USSR there was 1 drug addict per 1000 people (Zazulin, 2015), there are 5 injecting drug users per 1000 people these days, not counting those who use other types of drug. This suggests that the level of drug use since 1991 has increased by at least five times.

As with other drugs types, there are widely spread smoking mixtures, nasvay[3] and some inhalants classified as "intoxicating" substances. Currently, new psychoactive substances have appeared in the country, which is

---

3 *Naswār* (Pashto: نسوار, Cyrillic script: насвáр), also called *nās* (ناس; нáс) or *nasvay* (نسوای; насвай), is a moist, powdered tobacco dip consumed mostly in Afghanistan and surrounding countries. Naswar is stuffed in the floor of the mouth under the lower lip, or inside the cheek, for extended periods of time, usually for 15 to 30 minutes. It is similar to dipping tobacco and snus.

synthetic analogs mainly of cannabinoids, since they have a chemical structure similar to them. According to Botuzova (2014) the effect of new psychoactive substances is 5–10 times stronger than natural marijuana, and the addiction rate and withdrawal rate exceed those of heroin. Mainly psychoactive substances come from China in the form of smoking mixtures, the so-called "spice". Their feature is high profitability associated with low production costs since even small chemical labs can produce these psychoactive substances (Nogoibaev, 2010). There is a serious concern of some researchers such as Nogoibaev (2010), Botuzova (2014) that in the future, Kyrgyzstan might become a state of transit of these chemical drugs to Russia and Europe as it already happened with heroin from Afghanistan.

History of Early Institutional Care for Drug Treatment in USSR

Soviet Policy of drug addiction was not considered as an illness till the mid of 20 century. In the late 1960ies x when it was not possible to deny the existence of the problem Government used repressive methods by introducing the medical labour dispensaries. Medical-labor dispensary (MLD) was a type of medical correctional institution intended for those who, by a court decision, were sent for compulsory treatment for drug addiction and alcoholism. In fact, the MLD was a place of restriction of freedom, where the main method of treatment was the forced labor of the patient. At the same time, being in an MLD was not considered a prison term and made it possible to temporarily isolate alcoholics and drug users, drunken violators of public order without sending them to correctional facilities.

In 1967, an MLD was opened in the Kazakh SSR (Berzin, 2010). Then such institutions began to open in the RSFSR and other republics. On April 8, 1967, the Decree of the Presidium of the Supreme Soviet of the RSFSR "On the Compulsory Treatment and Labor Re-Education of Malicious Drunkards (Alcoholics)" was issued. It established that persons who "evade treatment or continue to drink after treatment, violate labor discipline, public order or the rules of a 'socialist coexistence'" should be sent to MLD. The term of stay in MLD was set from 6 months to 2 years; the decision to send him to it was made by a local judge. For escaping from a dispensary, criminal liability was established (Plotkin, 2015). Regulations on medical and labor dispensaries, adopted in the republics of the USSR, and regulations of the USSR Ministry of Internal Affairs extended the regime of compulsory treatment in MLD, close to the regime of serving a criminal sentence, to persons who had not committed criminal acts, which caused violations of their constitutional rights and freedoms. Most restrictions on the rights of persons held in dispensaries were not caused by the need for treatment. Persons were released from MLD, not for medical reasons but after the expiration of the period of detention established by the court.

As experts in the field of narcology noted, there is no reason to talk about the effectiveness of the "treatment" carried out in dispensaries. In addition, many "patients" began taking other drugs in MLD that cause a change in mental state (Plotkin, 2015). A significant part of the persons released from the MLD, immediately after the release, got drunk or used drugs to a severe degree of intoxication. The well-known psychiatrist and narcologist, director of the Institute for Mental Health Research Professor V. D. Mendelevich writes that "the effectiveness of MLD is close to zero. The fact is that MLDs are based on the principle of coercion – they brought people there, locked them up, but did not treat them. As a result, they came out of there and continued to take drugs" (Mendelevich, 2007). Director of the NSC Narcology Professor N. N. Ivanets points out a number of major shortcomings inherent in the organization of MLD: "poorly organized treatment process with minimal participation of psychotherapists; insufficient rehabilitation work with patients; organization of occupational therapy often without taking into account the characteristics of the patient's personality; often overly strict regime". He also writes that the percentage of long-term remissions after treatment in MLD was very low, even the opposite effect was often observed – an increase in the progression of the course of alcoholism and further desocialization of the patient. After the collapse of the Soviet Union, the MLD system was eliminated in most of the former Soviet republics. (Berzin, 2005) (UNODC/UNAIDS, 2022)

Narcological dispensary

The beginning of the organization of an independent narcological service in the Kyrgyz Republic dates back to 1976, when the first narcological dispensary was opened in Frunze, which became the main link in the system of narcological care, and subsequently, the main base of the current Republican Center for Narcology. However in the early 90s, after the collapse of Soviet Union, all governmental systems faced hard times. This situation was most dangerous because the health care system almost destroyed the existing structure and resources of the narcological services in the country. Only in 1996 by the decree of the Government of the Kyrgyz Republic dated No. December 23, 1996 from 1.01.1997, on the basis of the Chui regional drug dispensary and the Bishkek city drug treatment hospital, the Republican Narcology Center was organized, which became a focal point for coordinating public drug service in the country.

According to Shebardina, Nerubaieva and Dvinskykh (2017) the estimated number of injecting drug users is 25,000 people. This research study was based on sentinel surveillance and was conducted in 2015. The most commonly used drugs included anasha hashish cannabis), and heroin. Another finding of this study was that young people often prefer using volatile solvents, such as "Moment" glue, gasoline, and "carb". As synthetic drugs were used "salt" and "spice".

These days drug treatment, including rehabilitation of persons addicted to psychoactive substances, is provided by the state medical institutions of the Ministry of Health, medical institutions of the penitentiary system, private narcologists and non-governmental organizations.

Currently, the Republican Narcology Center is responsible following activities:

1. Coordination and methodological management of all structural divisions of the republic in drug treatment
2. Developing the guidelines for treatment methods based on the evidence medicine.
3. Provision of medical care in inpatient and outpatient settings and consultancy.
4. Management and implementation of harm reduction programs (methadone substitution therapy, needle and syringe exchange points, prevention of opioid overdose, etc.):
5. Implementation of rehabilitation and relapse prevention programs, work with codependents
6. Work of a preventive orientation program among the general population and children and youth.

Drug treatment Current time

The current situation of drug treatment services and facilities in the country was analyzed by Shebardina Anastasiya, Nerubaieva Iryna and Dvinskykh Natalya in the publication "the Needs and Gaps in treatment and rehabilitation for people who use drugs in selected countries of EECA" (2017). They found out that the supportive therapy for people who inject drugs in the Kyrgyz Republic has been realizing since 2002 with the use of the drug methadone hydrochloride.

The goals of agonist maintenance therapy are to stop or reduce the use of illicit opioids, to reduce the harm and health risks from a particular route of administration (for example, the risk of infections bysharing needles), and to reduce the social consequences of drug addiction. Treatment of patients with chemical dependencies may be divided into three stages:

1. Detoxification and relief of withdrawal symptoms with normalization of somatic and neurological disorders and correction of psychopathic disorders.
2. Recovery of metabolic disorders, behavioral disorders and normalization of the mental condition (including sleep).
3. Definition of the conditions preceding the relapse and prescribing anti-relapse treatment. Attention is paid to internal and external factors, leading to a spontaneous surge of craving for psychoactive substances.

The state drug treatment facilities offer:

1. Detoxification, which is carried out within inpatient and outpatient settings in all state drug treatment institutions.
2. Methadone maintenance therapy (MMT).
3. Inpatient medical and psychological rehabilitation and outpatient rehabilitation programs.

The rehabilitation services are provided at two state treatment facilities: rehabilitation outpatient office at the Republican Narcological Center in Bishkek and rehabilitation ward for 5 beds at the Osh Interdepartmental Narcological Center. Consultations of a narcologist and a psychologist are available at the local drug treatment offices countrywide.

Drug addiction treatment in the penitentiary system

There are 9 MMT sites in the penitentiary system, including two in the settings of the pre-trial detention centers, six at the closed correctional facilities, and one in the settings of settlement-type colony.

The rehabilitation program in the penitentiary system is represented by the "Atlantis" program, which is based on the Minnesota model for treatment of persons with drug dependence. There is also another program called "Clean Zone", available for those who successfully completed treatment in "Atlantis". (Azbel, 2017)

Drug addiction treatment in private clinics

In the Kyrgyz Republic the detoxification services are offered widely at the private clinics, but the only private clinic of the rehabilitation type is Dr. Nazaraliev's clinic [Best Drug Rehabilitation Treatment Centers | Nazaraliev Medical Center]. The cost of rehabilitation in the clinic can be as high as 1,695 EUR per month (even up to 6-8,00 USD). The average duration of rehabilitation there is 35–40 days, while in some cases, it can reach a year.

Non-governmental organizations providing rehabilitation services

Currently, there is one non-governmental rehabilitation center in Kyrgyzstan – Center Plus, operating in Osh on a self-financing basis. The center can accommodate up to 18 people. Rehabilitation program lasts up to 6 months.

The country has a large number of non-governmental organizations working in the field of providing services to people who use psychoactive substances. They include:

- Drop-in centers, which provide clients with information, medical and psychological services and social support;
- Social housing (providing clients with a place of residence);
- Half-way houses (providing clients with the opportunity to undergo a course of adaptation therapy, ensuring the participation of clients in the program of rehabilitation of dependence and further social adaptation)
- Social Bureau for PWID and PLWH released from prisons.

Recently, due to insufficient funding, some non-governmental organizations are closing.

The following rehabilitation models and approaches are the most widespread in the country:

- Based on therapeutic community (TC).
- Based on psychotherapeutic and rehabilitation self-help groups ("Alcoholics Anonymous" (AA), "Narcotics Anonymous" (NA)).
- Faith-based, operating as a therapeutic community within a religious context.

- Outpatient rehabilitation model (individual work of psychologist or psychiatrist with the client).

To assess the quality of treatment, in the health care system of the Kyrgyz Republic, the control functions are entrusted to the Obligatory Health Insurance Fund (OHIF), which is also a distributor of financial resources. Quality control of the services is also carried out by the licensing department of the Ministry of Health in accordance with the approved standards of services and established treatment quality indicators.

The licensing of private medical activities and the private health sector is carried out in accordance with the regulations and orders of the Ministry of Health of the Kyrgyz Republic. This licensing applies only to narcology and psychiatry and is not required for the services of social and psychological rehabilitation. Monitoring and evaluation of the quality of services in the non-governmental sector depends on the type of their activities and the requirements of the donor.

Methadone therapy in the country is carried out in accordance with the Clinical Protocol "Treatment of opioid dependence on the basis of methadone maintenance therapy" adopted by the Expert Council for the assessment of the quality of clinical guidelines / protocols and approved by Order of the Ministry of Health of the Kyrgyz Republic No. 372 dated June 30, 2015, and is carried out only in state medical institutions.

Role of social work in the field of treatment of drug dependence in the Kyrgyz Republic

After the collapse of the Soviet Union it was difficult to reorganize the governmental system; especially considering the economic crisis, poverty, and unemployment which were the main challenges for the newly reorganized government. Social support was in demand for the population, which barely survived due to the economic and political crisis. For the first time, the development of social protection policy in Kyrgyzstan received legal recognition in the Government Decree of December 1, 1993 No. 588 "On urgent measures to strengthen targeted social protection of the population". Social workers are a significant link in the system of social support. For Kyrgyzstan the preparation programs of social workers had been introduced at Bishkek Humanities University in 1994. In 1998, at the initiative of the Association of Social Workers and the Ministry of Labor and Social Protection, the Government of the country officially registered the profession – "Social Worker" (Musaeva, Orozaliev, 2014). However, the social worker's scope of duties was working mainly with the poor, disadvantaged, and vulnerable group of the population. Officially, the Ministry of Health has been engaging with drug treatment in Kyrgyzstan. Other state agencies have not been involved in drug treatment and social support. That brings us to the situation that medical workers are forced to perform some functions of social workers such as social support, legal help, etc. These days mainly NGOs are involved in this area but the decision on who will perform social work duties depends on the ability of the organization to recruit people. NGOs' social support was recognized as an important part of prevention programs, capable of providing quality support to substance abusers, PWID, positively influencing the adherence of participants to prevention programs in Kyrgyzstan. They work to strengthen the component of motivational counseling and involvement in harm reduction programs, as well as adherence to HIV treatment, STIs, and TB. The main goal of social support is to control and reduce the degree of behavioral risks about drug addiction that experience multiple problems and need a comprehensive approach to their solution. Social support allows a client with the help of a specialist to understand the problems, build a plan for finding their solution and get the necessary support in the process of gaining access to the necessary types of assistance. Thus, social support is a tool that creates the most favorable conditions for effective adaptation and interaction with social surroundings to change risky behavior. For example, social support for PWID has been provided by the AIDS Foundation East-West in the Kyrgyz Republic through partner non-governmental organizations since 2012 under the program "Bridging the Gaps: Health and Rights of Key Populations" funded by the Ministry of Foreign Affairs of the Netherlands. According to the results of research conducted by AFEW international *"Often many clients have nowhere to turn for help, they experience psychological barriers when contacting medical organizations that are not interested in providing services to key populations. They do not know where they can get tested for HIV, STI, and TB. Often they face housing difficulties, everyday disorders. Most are stereotyped about the opioid-substitution program and believe in the myths that are spreading among PWID about methadone. Therefore, the professionalism and competence of the worker are very important, since the subsequent trust and participation of PWID in the program depends on his behavior and decision"* (PF AFEW in Kyrgyzstan, 2015). These are the main reasons why we need to involve the social workers in the drug treatment and social support process from an institutionalized perspective because their role is crucial. Social worker assistantship is crucial in the process of rehabilitation concerning drug abusers, which is a system of social, psychological, educational, educational, legal, labor assistants aimed at the personal re-adaptation of patients, their resocialization, and reintegration into society.

Drug addiction and treatment in Kyrgyzstan has followed a spectacular trajectory over the past years that was largely influenced by governmental position, public perception of addiction, as well as economic, social and political movements. Drug addiction is widely studied from juridical disciplines perspective, they were most fruitful in terms laws, official documents, regulations and punishments. However there is a great lack of studies and publication from drug treatment perspectives. If there are some publications from medical subjects; there is gap on social support contribution to drug treatment, prevention and drug free life.

References

Anti-drug program of the Government of the Kyrgyz Republic, approved by the Decree of the Government of the Kyrgyz Republic dated January 27, 2014 No. 54. http://cbd.minjust.gov.kg

Azbel, L (2017): A qualitative assessment of an abstinence-oriented therapeutic community for prisoners with substance use disorders in Kyrgyzstan; HRJ 2017 Jul 10;14(1):43. DOI: 10.1186/s12954–017–0168–8

Berzin V. A. Legal problems of non-voluntary drug addiction Treatment of alcoholism // Narcologia.—2010.—5.— C. 75–86.

Botuzova I. Spice on the blood. More than 700 people were poisoned by a poisonous potion // St. Petersburg Vedomosti. 2014. October 10.

Clinical Guidelines for Methadone Substitution Maintenance Therapy for Opioid Dependence Syndrome No. 49 dated 11.11.10. http://www.rcn.kg

linical Guideline "Diagnostics, treatment of mental and behavioral disorders caused by the use of opioids" approved by order of the Ministry of Health of the Kyrgyz Republic No. 703 dated 12/25/2012. http://www.rcn.kg

Isakov T. Fight against drugs in Kyrgyzstan. – Bishkek: Ministry of Internal Affairs, 2001. – P.16

Kedeybaeva J., Bahramzhanova N. Development of social work in modern Kyrgyzstan B. 2021

Kurmanov K. Drug addiction (1989). Criminal – legal and criminological problems. – P.19.

Kuttubaev T.K. (2017): Analysis of the Drug Situation in Kyrgyz Republic

Nogoibaev B.B. Drug situation: analysis, diagnosis, prognosis. Bishkek, 2010. 332 p.

Nogoibaev B.B. Fundamentals of drug safety. Bishkek: Altyn Print, 2014. 304 p.

On measures to regulate the trade in narcotic drugs, Decree of the Council of People's Commissars of the USSR, Decree of the Central Executive Committee of the USSR accepted on May 23, 1928, SZ USSR, 1928, N 33, item 290

Mendelevich V.D. Involuntary (compulsory) and alternative treatment of drug addiction: controversial issues of theory and practice // Narcology. – 2007. – No. 7. – S. 66–75. – ISSN 1682–8313.

Moller L, Karymbaeva S, Subata E, Kiaer T. (2009). Evaluation of patients in opioid substitution therapy in the Kyrgyz Republic, WHO Europe.

Musaeva N., Orozaliev E. Philosophy of Social work. Bishkek. "Gazeta KG", 2014. – 311 p.

Regulations on the procedure for licensing private medical activities in the Kyrgyz Republic approved by order of the Ministry of Health of the Kyrgyz Republic No. 337 dated April 21, 2017. http://cbd.minjust.gov.kg, http://med.kg, http://www.ksmi.kg/

Regulations on the Narcological Rehabilitation Center, approved by order of the Ministry of Health of the Kyrgyz Republic No. 65 dated 12.02.2004. http://www.rcn.kg

Plotkin F.B. New trends in Russian narcology: a return to the old coercive methods of coercive treatment // Independent Psychiatric Journal. – 2015. – No. 4. – S. 13–24.

PF "AIDS Foundation East-West in the Kyrgyz Republic" Assessment of the quality of social support for people who use drugs in the Kyrgyz Republic. "Bridging the Gaps: The Health and Rights of Key Populations" Bishkek, 2015

Tugelbaeva B.G., Khamzaeva D.D. (2017) Istoriya i sovremennoe sostoyanie narkosituatsii v Kyrgyzstane [History and current state of the drug situation in Kyrgyzstan]. Voprosy rossiiskogo i mezhdunarodnogo prava [Matters of Russian and International Law], 7 (12A), pp. 150–158.

Shebardina A, Nerubaieva I and Dvinskykh N (2017) Needs and gaps in treatment and rehabilitation for people who use drugs in selected countries of eeca

Standards for the provision of medical services for injecting drug users, approved by order No. 494 of October 8, 2010: Standard for conducting detoxification therapy for opioid withdrawal in the inpatient department of the Republican Narcology Center; Standard for opioid overdose prevention using naloxone; The standard for conducting rehabilitation activities for people with opioid dependence. http://www.rcn.kgЗакон «О лекарственных средствах». http://cbd.minjust.gov.kg/act/view/ru-ru/513?cl=ru-ru

UNODC/UNAIDS (2022): Compulsory Drug Treatment and Rehabilitation in East and Southwest Asia; Vienna/Geneva, February 2022

Zabransky, T., & Mravcik, V. (Eds.). (2019). The 2019 Regional Report on the Drug Situation in Central Asia [Региональный обзор о наркоситуации в Центральной Азии 2019]. Bishkek/ Prague: CADAP 6/ResAd

Zelichenko Alexander. The Afghan Drug Expansion of the 1990s, ed. 2nd, add. – B.: Continent, 2004. – 364 p. Circulation 100 copies.

Zhirnov E. The case of Soviet drug cartels 07.10.2013 Journal "Kommersant Money"

1.3. Uzbekistan: History of drug addiction and treatment in Uzbekistan

Akhatjon Nasullaev

Introduction

Drug use and drug addiction are public health issues which impose serious implications for development and security. Collectively, smoking, alcohol and illicit drug use kills 11.8 million people each year. This is more than the number of deaths from all cancers (Roth et.al., 2018). Drug use disorders are associated with an increased prevalence of other diseases such as HIV / AIDS, hepatitis, tuberculosis and cardiovascular disease, as well as phenomena such as suicide and overdose deaths. According to the World Drug Report (2019), 2.21 million between ages 15 and 64 has used drugs at least once in Central Asia and South Caucasus in 2017. Estimations state that around 338,000 people in the region inject drugs and around 7 % of them live with HIV[1].

Uzbekistan being one of the countries of Central Asia although shows decreasing trend, remains vulnerable with the existence of drug users and addicts in the country. If the number of officially registered drug users increased by 800 % between 1991 and 2005 in Uzbekistan (Godinho et al., 2005), this number decreased twice between 2007–2016 (from 19 868 to 10 505 respectively) according to the Ministry of Health of the Republic of Uzbekistan. National Information and Analytical Center for Drug Control under the Cabinet of Ministers of the Republic of Uzbekistan gives following comparative table to describe overall situation in the country for the years 2014 and 2015:

	2014	**2015**
Number of drug addicts registered with health authorities	14 692	13 218
Number of drug addicts who inject drugs	5110	3825
of them patients with heroin addiction	4758	3517
Number of HIV-infected drug users	5377	5665

---

1 UNAIDS (2018) Country factsheets.

Several recent reports highlight the decreasing number of drug addicts registered with dispensaries – 5,698 in 2019 (2018 – 6,142).[2] However, the number of drug addicts identified and registered with dispensaries increased slightly – 1,164 (1,126). The growth of the indicator was observed in the city of Tashkent, Bukhara and Tashkent region[3].

The above-mentioned reports also state that in the structure of drug addiction, the number of cannabinoid addicts prevails – 3,982 (4169) or 69.9 % (67.9 %) of the total number of registered users, and those dependent on drugs of the opium group accounted for 1418 (1684) or 24.9 % (27, four%). The number of heroin users decreased by 1.8 times – 536 (979) or 9.4 % (15.9 %).

Analysis of age and gender characteristics of drug addicts registered in 2016 shows the increase in the number of patients aged 40 and above with prevailing number of men[4].

If in Uzbekistan the first case of detection of the drug "spice" was registered in 2015, so far, several dozen new types of substances have been discovered in the illegal circulation. According to the UNODC, over 60 different types of synthetic drugs have been identified in the CA region. Their relative cheapness, complexity of detection and identification, variability of species and forms pose a serious threat to the health and well-being of the population, especially young people.

The data described above come from National Health Authorities of the Republic. A country report of European Monitoring Center for Drugs and Drug Addiction states that, so far, no study on the prevalence of drug use among the general population has been conducted in the Republic of Uzbekistan[5].

The most recent study which was performed by United Nations Office on Drugs and Crime (UNODC) in 2006 to assess the extent of alcohol, tobacco and drug use among 5,851 children born in 1990 (students in the 9th grade of 6 regions of Uzbekistan) revealed low levels of drug use. 0.5 % respondents indicated that they had consumed a drug (cannabis, inhalants) once or twice in their life.

---

2 https://yumh.uz/ru/news_detail/210.

3 http://uzbekistan-geneva.ch/informaciya-o-narkosituacii-v-respublike-uzbekistan-v-2019-godu.html.

4 Information bulletin on drug related situation. The Central Asian region. Tashkent, Baktria press, 2017.

5 Overview of the drug situation in Uzbekistan (2014) | www.emcdda.europa.eu.

1. Drug addiction treatment in Uzbekistan

In 1994 a national anti-drug strategy was developed in Uzbekistan with establishment of two entities: State Commission of the Republic of Uzbekistan on Drug Control and its executive apparatus and the National Information and Analytical Center for Drug Control under the Cabinet of Ministers of the Republic of Uzbekistan. Several laws, decrees, resolutions and programs have been adopted in order to regulate anti-drug policy of the government. For example, Law of the Republic of Uzbekistan No. 813-I "On narcotic drugs and psychotropic substances" dated August 19, 1999; Law of the Republic of Uzbekistan No. 644 "On prevention and treatment of narcological diseases" dated October 27, 2020 define main directions of anti-drug policy.

In order to further implement comprehensive measures to combat drug abuse and their illicit trafficking, improve the system of providing drug treatment medical care, and provide legal support for anti-drug activities "A Program of Comprehensive Measures to Combat Drug Abuse and Illicit Trafficking for 2016–2020" was adopted.

Article 13 of the Law of the Republic of Uzbekistan No. 644 "On prevention and treatment of narcological diseases" defines health care institutions providing narcological assistance to the population. Narcological assistance to the population is provided by narcological institutions of the state health care system or private medical institutions licensed to carry out medical activities in the specialization "Narcology".

Narcological dispensaries are organized in the Republic of Karakalpakstan, regions, the city of Tashkent, as well as large cities of the country as independent medical and preventive institutions of the republican, regional, city or inter-district level.

Narcological assistance on an outpatient basis is provided by narcological offices organized in the structure of central district (city) multidisciplinary polyclinics.

Narcological assistance in inpatient conditions is provided by the Republican Specialized Scientific and Practical Medical Center for Narcology, narcological dispensaries, narcological departments of neuropsychiatric institutions, narcological hospitals for compulsory treatment, departments for compulsory treatment of narcological dispensaries.

Emergency medical care for acute intoxication with psychoactive substances is provided by territorial centers of emergency medical care.

According to this law, the state guarantees emergency medical care for acute intoxication with psychoactive substances, alcoholic and intoxication psychoses caused using psychoactive substances; and consultative and diagnostic, medical, psychoprophylactic, rehabilitation, social assistance in outpatient and inpatient conditions. The law also sets out conditions for compulsory treatment.

The government established "trust points" within public health facilities in order to reduce rate of HIV infection. These anonymous public health facilities provide counselling on consequences of drug abuse, HIV, sexually transmitted infections for the vulnerable groups.

2. Literature review

Literature on treatment of drug consumption and addiction with a special focus on Uzbekistan is diverse.

The paper by Turaeva and Engmann (2014) investigates how patterns of drug consumption reflect religious, historical and political influences and are also shaped by the availability of a drug. The authors argue that drug consumption has a long tradition in present day Uzbekistan. If wine played a prominent role in ancient times, due to tightening rule of Islam it was prohibited and it was replaced by opium. Within recent decades there is a shift of drug using patterns: drinking opium – smoking opium – injecting opium/heroin – combinations of both heroin and pharmaceutical remedies. The authors conclude that risk of opium consumption has been decreased because of societal reasoning by elderly people explaining harm of the drugs.

Shigakova (2015) discusses effects of ethno-cultural and socio-economic factors on prevalence of the opium addiction among Uzbek indigenous inhabitants and Slavs born and residing in Uzbekistan. "Positive social influence confirms significant role of the community dominant personalities, parents, wives and the clergy in prevention and spread of drug addiction as well as in treatment and medical-social rehabilitation of drug addicts". The authors note that national heritages, adherence to religion and cultural values have a significant role in counter-narcotic resistance.

Latypov (2011) reviews the development of early Soviet drug treatment approaches by focusing on the struggle for disciplinary power between leading social and mental hygienists and clinical psychiatrists. The research highlights evolution of different drug treatment strategies in Soviet countries under the political and ideological environment.

One strand of research discusses relationship between drug use and HIV infection in Uzbekistan. Sanchez et al. (2006) state that nearly 30 % of a sample of injection drug users (IDUs) was HIV positive in a recent study from Uzbekistan. Todd et al. (2007) describe prevalence and correlates of sexual risk behaviors among injection drug users in Tashkent, Uzbekistan. They confirm that risky sexual behaviors are common and interrelated with risky injection habits among IDUs in Tashkent, Uzbekistan, representing a continued threat of infection with HIV and other blood-borne agents.

Similarly, Claire Thorne, et al. (2010) reveal prevalence of hepatitis C virus and syphilis among IDUs which exceeds 60 % in Tajikistan and Uzbekistan, 70 % in Kazakhstan. According to the study, "female IDUs are particularly vulnerable to infection with HIV, HCV, and STIs, because of the exchange of sex for drugs or money and risky injecting behaviors".

Multi-level combination prevention interventions should be developed and adopted with an attention to sexual partners and risk networks of IDUs, aiming at early detection of HIV, timely enrollment in HIV care, and retention in HIV care (Boltaev et al., 2013). Schluger et al. (2013) suggest integration of TB services, HIV care, and substance abuse treatment programs is needed urgently to allow efficient and effective diagnosis and treatment of these conditions in a coordinated manner.

Longfield et al. (2005) examine drug use among Tadjik and Uzbek youth. They conclude that youth are very well informed about negative consequences of drug use. Even if they show tolerance for certain types of substances, such as alcohol and tobacco, risk perception for heroin or other types of drugs is low.

3. Role of NGOs in drug addiction treatment in Uzbekistan

To date around 10,000 NGOs exist in Uzbekistan. Given the fact that several obstacles are reported by NGOs in the country, such as *long administrative procedures for registration, barriers in the process of carrying out their statutory activities*, the number of NGOs in Uzbekistan almost doubled in 2018 comparing to 2006[6]. However, it should be noted that this number also includes branches of political parties, trade unions and representative branches of NGOs operating at the republican level. NGOs which are acting in healthcare constitutes only 2 % of the total amount[7].

In fact, NGOs play a significant role in aiding governments by bridging state agencies and local populations in providing adequate healthcare

---

6 Development of civil society institutions in Uzbekistan: figures and facts 2017.
7 Analytical report of Center for the development of civil society "The state of the "third sector" in Uzbekistan: reality and development prospects" 2018.

(Gomez-Jauregui 2004; Johnson 2009). In Uzbekistan, state supports activities of NGOs by providing financial and technical assistance through different grant programs. International donor organizations also have an important role in developing capacity of NGOs in providing health and other social welfare services.

Activities carried out by NGOs in the field of drug addiction is diverse. They participate in voluntary health and welfare programs oriented to prevention, control and rehabilitation. Main activities include organizing health educational campaigns, outreach to vulnerable people, counselling, training health professionals working with drug addicts.

NGOs work closely with government entities in HIV prevention programs (Wolfe et al., 2008). Several successful cases have been documented in which effective cooperation of NGOs with *mahallas* is highlighted (Amirkhanian et al., 2004). Mahalla is a century-old system of neighborhood committee in Uzbekistan, which is unique structure by its nature. In fact, activities of NGOs are strongly connected with government entities and self-governed bodies like mahallas which explains joint actions for meeting societal needs.

In conclusion, this work tried to describe the general tendencies related to drug addiction and its treatment in Uzbekistan. The role of NGOs in drug addiction treatment was also briefly reported. It is also noteworthy that there is a large window for future research on how NGOs specifically deal with drug addiction. Future works will be dedicated to this topic more in depth.

References:

"Roth, G. A., Abate, D., Abate, K. H., Abay, S. M., Abbafati, C., Abbasi, N., … & Abdollahpour, I. (2018). Global, regional, and national age-sex-specific mortality for 282 causes of death in 195 countries and territories, 1980–2017: a systematic analysis for the Global Burden of Disease Study 2017. *The Lancet*, 392(10159), 1736-1788".

Amirkhanian, Y.A., Kelly, J.A., Benotsch, E.G., Somlai, A.M., Brown, K.D., Fernandez, M.I., Opgenorth, K.M. (2004). HIV prevention nongovernmental organizations in central and eastern europe: programs, resources and challenges. Cent Eur J Publ Health, 12 (1): 12-1

Boltaev, A., El-Bassel, N., Deryabinaa, A., Terlikbaeva, A., Gilbert, L., Hunt, T., Primbetova, Sh., Strathdee, S. (2013). Scaling up HIV prevention efforts targeting people who inject drugs in Central Asia: A review of key challenges and ways forward. Drug and Alcohol Dependence, 132, S41–S47. doi:10.1016/j.drugalcdep.2013.07.033

Claire Thorne, et al. (2010). Central Asia: Hotspot in the Worldwide HIV Epidemic. The Lancet Infectious Diseases, 10(7):479-88. doi: 10.1016/S1473-3099(10)701 18-3

Godinho, J., Renton, A., Vinogradov, V., Novotyn, T., Rivers, M.J., Gotsadze, G., & Bravo, M. (2005). Reversing the Tide: Priorities for HIV/AIDS Prevention in Central Asia. Washington DC: The World Bank.

Gomez-Jauregui, J. (2004). The Feasibility of Government Partnerships with NGOs in the Reproductive Health Field in Mexico', Reproductive Health Matters, 12, 24.

Johnson, E. (2009). Authoritarian Regimes and Nongovernmental Organizations: Transitions in Health Care Provision in Central Asia (Seattle, WA, University of Washington).

Latypov, A.B. The Soviet doctor and the treatment of drug addiction: "A difficult and most ungracious task". *Harm Reduct J* **8**, 32 (2011). https://doi.org/10.1186/1 477-7517-8-32

Longfield, Kim, Amara Robinson, Rob Gray, and Chris Jones. 2005. Youth Perspectives on Drug Use, Heroin, and Risk for HIV/AIDS in Tajikistan and Uzbekistan, Central Asia. Washington, DC. Population Services International: Working Paper no. 65.

Sanchez, J.L., Todd, C.S., Bautista, C.T., Botros, B.A., Khakimov, M.M., Giyasova, G.M., Yakubov, S.K., Abdulaeva, M.A., Saad, M.D., Graham, R.R., Carr, J.K., Earhart, K.C., 2006. High HIV prevalence and risk factors among injection drug users in Tashkent, Uzbekistan, 2003–2004. Drug Alcohol Depend. 82 (Suppl. 1), S15–S22.

Scaling up HIV prevention efforts targeting people who inject drugs in Central Asia: A review of key challenges and ways forward. Drug and Alcohol Dependence 132:41–47

Schluger et al. (2013). Tuberculosis, drug use and HIV infection in Central Asia: An urgent need for attention. Drug and Alcohol dependence, 32S (2013) S32–S36.

Shigakova F., A. (2015). Transcultural aspects of opium addiction in the Republic of Uzbekistan. European science review, 106-110.

Todd, C. S., Earhart, K. C., Botros, B. A., Khakimov, M. M., Giyasova, G. M., Bautista, C. T., ... Sanchez, J. L. (2007). Prevalence and correlates of risky sexual behaviors among injection drug users in Tashkent, Uzbekistan. AIDS Care, 19(1), 122–129. doi:10.1080/09540120600852150

Turaeva, M., Engmann B. (2014). Drug consumption in Central Asia with a focus on Uzbekistan in the mirror of region's history. British journal of applied science and technology, 4 (13), 1882-1890.

Wolfe, D., Elovich, R., Boltaev, A., & Pulatov, D. (2008). HIV in Central Asia: Tajikistan, Uzbekistan and Kyrgyzstan. Public Health Aspects of HIV/AIDS in Low- and Middle-Income Countries, 557–581. doi:10.1007/978-0-387-72711-0 _25

1.4. China: History of development of addiction treatment social work in China

Hang Su

The origin of addiction treatment social work

In the mid-1950s, about 90 % of the prisoners in Hong Kong's prisons were addicted to drugs. The Prisons Department (formerly known as the Correctional Services Department) took the lead in opening the first compulsory drug treatment center in Tai Lam Tong prison in 1958. As a result, the Hong Kong Prisons Department has become a pioneer in all organized drug treatment (Fan, 2009). In addition to providing comprehensive medical services to drug abusers, the Hong Kong Prisons Department's compulsory treatment program will also help drug abusers to get rid of their psychological and emotional dependence on drugs through work therapy (physical and outdoor work) and individual or group counseling. Within 12 months after their release, a rehabilitation counselor will be responsible for arranging their occupation and residence, and they will be under the supervision of the rehabilitation counselor. In addition, there are a considerable number of NGOs and social workers involved (Fang, 2006).

Macao stopped compulsory drug treatment service in 1990 and replaced it with voluntary outpatient service. social workers infiltrate into the whole process of treatment, from "professional treatment group" in outpatient treatment to social psychological counseling, providing professional assist, helping drug abusers return to society and family, dealing with family problems, providing family counseling, and follow up and supervise those who have applied for assistance. After returning to society, the Social Work Bureau of Macao actively advocated the establishment of "self-help organizations" to consolidate the rehabilitation effect (Yang, 2005).

The initial stage (1994–1998)

Baotou City in Inner Mongolia is a model of China's "non-drug community". The drug problem in this city used to be very serious. After 1994, the whole city took drug prohibition and rehabilitation as the breakthrough point, carried out an activity of creating "non-drug community", generally established and implemented the responsibility system of drug control work, which was vertical to the assistance and education group and horizontal to all grass-roots units within the jurisdiction, and formed a situation in which the whole people participated in the fight against drugs (Fan, 2009).

In March 1996, the National Drug Control Commission cooperated with the United Nations Economic and Social Council for Asia and the Pacific to implement the national strategic project of community-based drug demand reduction and AIDS prevention in Yunnan. The core of Yunnan Community detoxification model is "five hearts", namely sincerity, love, confidence, patience and heart exchanging: use "sincerity" and "love" to educate and save drug abusers, use "patience" and "confidence" to light the fire of drug abusers' lives and raise the sails of their lives, use "heart exchanging" to arouse drug abusers' confidence and sense of responsibility, and help them complete the active transformation from "Want me to quit" to "I want to quit" (Fan, 2009).

However, the activities of "non-drug community" basically follow the traditional way of the government to manage the society by administrative means, and the enthusiasm and participation of citizens and social organizations have not really involved.

The exploration stage (1998–2006)

In September 1998, Yunnan Daytop drug dependence treatment and rehabilitation center was established in Kunming. Daytop community therapy mode originated in the United States, and was founded in 1953 (Tang & Huang, 2008; Yang et al., 2002). It is the first professional institution in China to treat drug abusers and provide aftercare services from the perspective of sociology, psychology, behavior, clinical medicine, preventive medicine and other disciplines in treatment community mode. In 2001, the Department of social work of Yunnan University cooperated with Daytop drug dependence treatment and rehabilitation center. The former provided training for the staff, while the latter provided practice site and supervision (Li & Ma, 2014).

Based on the successful experience of Yunnan Daytop treatment community, Xiaogan drug dependence treatment center established Xiaogan home, the first drug rehabilitation community in Hubei Province in 2000. Besides, some compulsory drug treatment centers try to introduce the community therapy mode into the compulsory drug treatment system. For example, the improved community therapy model of Jinhua drug treatment center in Zhejiang Province and the Sunflower treatment community of Beijing drug treatment center, which was officially established in November 2003. They were all based on American Daytop mode, which were an important exploration to combine the treatment community with the practice of compulsory detoxification in China. They are similar to Yunnan Daytop treatment community in operation concept, operation organization and operation characteristics, such as adopting hierarchical management structure, carrying out various forms of group activities, diversifying behavior correction tools, etc (Du, 2002). However, the establishment of Daytop treatment community mode needs a lot of investment in human, financial and material aspects, but it can only accommodate a limited number of residents, which limits its large-scale promotion; in addition, the high loss rate is also an important limitation of the treatment community mode.

Since 2003, Shanghai has introduced the concept and method of social work in the field of drug control and rehabilitation, recruited and trained the team of social workers, thus taking the lead in the innovation of drug control social work system in China. The basic experience of Shanghai drug treatment social work system is creating a new model of community drug rehabilitation, which is "government leading, community independent operation, social participation".

At present, the definition of "drug treatment social worker" in Shanghai is as follows: professional personnel of non-governmental organizations who have certain scientific knowledge, methods and skills of drug treatment and social work, and provide life care, rehabilitation assistance, employment guidance, legal advisory services and behavior supervision to the working objects in a certain period of time (Fan & Lv, 2005; Fan et al., 2008).

In August 2003, Shanghai took the lead in providing drug treatment social work services in Pudong, Xuhui, Luwan and Zhabei districts. In December 2003, Shanghai Ziqiang Social Service Association, the first community drug treatment organization in China, was established. In August 2004, drug treatment social work service was launched in 19 districts and counties of the city. In accordance with the idea of "government leading, community independent operation and social participation", drug treatment social workers actively explore community rehabilitation mode to help drug abusers return to society and improve their social functions (Fan, 2009).

Under the concept and framework of "government purchasing services", Shanghai Ziqiang Social Service Corporation was registered as a "private non enterprise organization" on December 22, 2003, and under supervision by the office of Shanghai Drug Control Commission (Zhao et al., 2011). In November 2003, Shanghai Drug Control Commission signed a government service procurement contract with Shanghai Ziqiang Social Service Corporation to purchase community drug treatment services of social workers at the standard of 40000 yuan per social worker. Shanghai Ziqiang Social Service Association is the operational entity of drug treatment social work (Fan et al., 2008). Ziqiang Social Service Corporation began to recruit the first batch of social workers since October 2003. The scale of drug treatment social workers is about 400 (Service, 2003). The source of these social workers team is relatively complicated, which can be divided into three parts: some of them come from social recruitment, some from old public security, and some from prison bureau (Fan, 2005; Fan & Lv, 2005).

On October 30, 2007, Zhongzhi Community Service Association was established in Pudong District of Shanghai. The newly established Zhongzhi Community Service Association is a combination of three Pudong workstations: Ziqiang, Xinhang and Yangguang, with 169 full-time social workers (Service, 2007). By 2009, Ziqiang Social Service Association has established 19 drug treatment social work stations at the district level and 195 drug treatment social workers at the community level (Zhong, 2010). At present, Zhongzhi has set up social work teams, three project teams and one social work station in 36 towns and cities in Pudong. There are more than 280 social workers, 80 % of whom have bachelor's degrees and 80 % of whom have professional qualifications such as social workers or psychological counselors.

Zhangjiagang and Suzhou have also set up Ziqiang social service agencies, and Kunming and other cities have set up drug treatment social work teams. In addition, social work departments in Yunnan, Hunan, Guangdong and other places start from practical teaching, and carry out drug treatment social work practice in voluntary drug treatment hospitals, compulsory drug treatment centers and communities. Under the guidance of professional teachers and internship supervision, social work students in schools work as volunteers or interns (Zhong, 2010).

The establishment of drug treatment social workers marks the transformation of community drug treatment from simple government administrative action to social action, mobilizing all social forces to participate in drug treatment.

The transition stage (2006–2007)

In order to strengthen the construction of professional and technical personnel of social work, standardize their professional behaviors and improve their ability, on July 20, 2006, the Ministry of Personnel and the Ministry of Civil Affairs jointly issued the Interim Provisions on the evaluation of the professional level of social workers and the measures for examining the professional level of assistant social workers and social workers. The publication of these two documents indicates that the scope of professionalization and specialization of social work has expanded from the local level to the overall level, and the level of professionalization and specialization has risen from the regional level to the central level. The professionalization and specialization of social work has been accelerated.

On December 29, 2007, the 31st meeting of the Standing Committee of the 10th National People's Congress deliberated and adopted the Drug Control Law of the People's Republic of China, which came into force on June 1, 2008. The law has a new formulation on the mode of drug treatment in China. For the first time, it explicitly puts forward a new mode of drug treatment, which takes community drug treatment as the main body, and compulsory and voluntary drug treatment as the supplement. Since then, the legal status of "community treatment" has been confirmed. The law undoubtedly promoted the institutionalization and legalization of drug rehabilitation social work (Li & Ma, 2014; Zhang, 2011).

The promotion stage (from 2007 to now)

On October 25, 2007, the Shenzhen government issued the "opinions of the Shenzhen Municipal Committee and the Shenzhen Municipal People's Government on strengthening the construction of social work and promoting the development of social work" and seven supporting documents (referred to as the "1+7" document). These series of documents have made specific provisions on how to strengthen the construction of social work team, the evaluation of social work professional level, the education and training of social workers, the setting of social work professional posts, the salary of social workers, the role of non-governmental organizations in social work, public financial security, and the linkage mechanism between social workers and volunteers, initially formed a "Shenzhen characteristics of the social work system"(Tang, 2008).

The specific measures of Shenzhen to promote the development of social work for drug treatment are as follows: 1) actively expand the social work service field including drug control; 2) set up professional posts for social work in drug control departments, with one social worker for every 70 drug abusers. Shenzhen's practice has a demonstration effect in the whole country (Fan, 2009).

In June 2008, Suzhou Ziqiang Social Service Association of Jiangsu Province was established, and the government funded the purchase of social work services to recruit drug treatment social workers. In Shenzhen, Zhejiang, Shandong and other places, drug treatment social work was also set up, and these social workers were full-time. The social work major of Yunnan Police Officer College began to recruit students in 2011 to cultivate professional drug treatment social workers (Li, 2012).

Guangdong Lianzhong Social Worker Service for Drug Rehabilitation was established in 2008 and has since evolved into the Lianzhong model. It has made significant efforts in personnel training, launching a management trainee training program, constructing a social work training center, and signing a joint doctoral training agreement on drug control with East China University of Science and Technology's School of Social and Public Administration. Addiction social workers' standards and professional development will be aided by the continuing export of expertise and talent. (Mai,2019)

With the deepening of the legalization and standardization of drug control work, the main tasks of drug treatment social work in this period are: to explore the community drug treatment mode, reduce the relapse rate through scientific, systematic and professional social work, help drug abusers return to society; to remind people of staying away from drugs through publicity and education, to prevent the first drug use; to carry out professional education and training of drug treatment social work; to cultivate professional drug treatment social workers and build professional drug treatment social work team. The characteristics of the professional development stage of drug control social work are: government led promotion, independent operation of associations, multi-party participation of society; combination of drug control work and social work; transition from non specialization and non standardization to specialization and standardization, so as to make drug treatment social work more professional, legal and standardized (Zhang & Wang, 2014).

The management of complex problems of and related to substance abuse and addictions requires comprehensive approaches based on interdisciplinary teamwork, according to a large body of data. Drug addiction has been classed as "psychiatric" under "clinical medicine" after the consensus that drug addiction is recurring encephalopathy. Addiction treatment necessitates a multidisciplinary approach that includes medicine, sociology, psychology, and other disciplines. (Chu, 2020) Community drug prohibition service stations staffed by doctors, paramedics, and social workers have been constructed in numerous Chinese cities to assist opioid drug users. They provide drug users with treatment, counselling, and assistance in order to help them reintegrate into society and find work. Meanwhile, psychiatrists can increase the professional training of drug rehabilitation institution personnel in social psychological counseling and related medical information to improve their professional skill and psychological adjustment ability to deal with drug abusers' atypical behaviors. (Lai, 2020)

With the rapid development of Internet cloud data, relying on the progress of algorithms and big data, the barriers of traditional data management mode are being broken. The "Internet +" became a national strategy in the 2015 government work report. In August of that year, the National Narcotics Control Commission put the community rehabilitation work on the agenda and actively promoted community drug rehabilitation to networking and intellectualization by creating of a cloud data local area network as a communication and cooperation platform for community drug treatment and community rehabilitation work. It can effectively realize the collection, management and timely update of information, establish the automatic analysis model, ensure the community drug treatment and community rehabilitation work, and realize the real-time dynamic maintenance of the network. Open up the data channel between the community and the public security, civil affairs, health and other departments, integrate the information of personnel, family background, social activities and other information, so as to realize the dynamic real-time maintenance of information and the timeliness and accuracy of data. Then use big data and cloud computing technology to strengthen the integration and application of information resources, and create a "data fence" according to the actual situation of community drug treatment and community rehabilitation personnel. Create an automatic analysis model of information, implement the integral early warning system, study and judge, and generate individualized and differentiated management and control help and education programs (Li et al., 2018).

According to the characteristics of community drug treatment and community rehabilitation, a personalized database is designed, which can collect, store and process all kinds of data generated by the equipment and staff in the work of community drug treatment and community rehabilitation, so that all staff can input the data at any time and complete the query and transfer of information. It can establish data base for modeling and analysis. According to the actual needs of detoxification and rehabilitation personnel, a wearable device similar to smart bracelet is customized for community detoxification and community rehabilitation personnel. It can measure and monitor the temperature, heartbeat, sleep duration, geographical location and other information of detoxification and rehabilitation personnel in real time, and timely transmit them to the cloud database, so as to timely understand the real-time situation of community detoxification and rehabilitation personnel. Some hidden clues can also be displayed, such as the contact object, the activity track of drug abusers, etc (Li et al., 2018).

Main problems in the development of social work for drug treatment in China

1. More attention to drug control than rehabilitation;
2. More attention to detoxification than rehabilitation;
3. More attention to physical and psychological rehabilitation than social rehabilitation;
4. Opinions on drug abusers and their social security;
5. Scientificity and rationality of the evaluation criteria for drug treatment achievements;
6. Specialization of social workers for drug treatment;
7. On the independent operation of drug treatment organizations under the background of strong government;

Potential research questions in future

1. Compare the historical development process of drug treatment social work in different countries;
2. Make standardized protocol of psychotherapy training courses for social workers to improve their professional level;
3. Differences in drug treatment policy, the degree of government participation and the voice of non-governmental organizations in different countries;
4. Family treatment or group treatment may be useful to encourage more drug abusers to actively participate in drug treatment.

Social Work Development in Shanghai and role of NGOs

Since 2003, Shanghai has introduced the concept and method of social work in the field of drug control and rehabilitation, recruited and trained the team of social workers, thus taking the lead in the innovation of drug control social work system in China. The basic experience of Shanghai drug treatment social work system is creating a new model of community drug rehabilitation, which is "government leading, community independent operation, social participation".

At present, the definition of "drug treatment social worker" in Shanghai is as follows: professional personnel of non-governmental organizations who have certain scientific knowledge, methods and skills of drug treatment and social work, and provide life care, rehabilitation assistance, employment guidance, legal advisory services and behavior supervision to the working objects in a certain period of time (Fan & Lv, 2005; Fan et al., 2008).

In August 2003, Shanghai took the lead in providing drug treatment social work services in Pudong, Xuhui, Luwan and Zhabei districts. In December 2003, Shanghai Ziqiang Social Service Association, the first community drug treatment organization in China, was established. In August 2004, drug treatment social work service was launched in 19 districts and counties of the city. In accordance with the idea of "government leading, community independent operation and social participation", drug treatment social workers actively explore community rehabilitation mode to help drug abusers return to society and improve their social functions (Fan, 2009).

Under the concept and framework of "government purchasing services", Shanghai Ziqiang Social Service Corporation was registered as a "private non enterprise organization" on December 22, 2003, and under supervision by the office of Shanghai Drug Control Commission (Zhao et al., 2011). In November 2003, Shanghai Drug Control Commission signed a government service procurement contract with Shanghai Ziqiang Social Service Corporation to purchase community drug treatment services of social workers at the standard of 40000 yuan per social worker. Shanghai Ziqiang Social Service Association is the operational entity of drug treatment social work (Fan et al., 2008). Ziqiang Social Service Corporation began to recruit the first batch of social workers since October 2003. The scale of drug treatment social workers is about 400 (Service, 2003). The source of these social workers' teams is relatively complicated, which can be divided into three parts: some of them come from social recruitment, some from old public security, and some from prison bureau (Fan, 2005; Fan & Lv, 2005).

On October 30, 2007, Zhongzhi Community Service Association was established in Pudong District of Shanghai. The newly established Zhongzhi Community Service Association is a combination of three Pudong workstations: Ziqiang, Xinhang and Yangguang, with 169 full-time social workers (Service, 2007). By 2009, Ziqiang Social Service Association had established 19 drug treatment social work stations at the district level and 195 drug treatment social workers at the community level (Zhong, 2010). At present, Zhongzhi has set up social work teams, three project teams and one social work station in 36 towns and cities in Pudong. There are more than 280 social workers, 80 % of whom have bachelor's degrees and 80 % of whom have professional qualifications such as social workers or psychological counselors.

Together with Siqi Community Service Association in Fengxian District, Shanghai has formed three major community drug treatment service institutions to provide social work services and support for drug users in the city.

In addition, NGOs also include the anonymous drug users association (Narcotics Anonymous, NA) in Shanghai. NA is a non-profit organization whose members are all drug users. The method of detoxification is to help each other, so as to achieve the purpose of rehabilitation. NA doesn't care what kind of drugs members use, nor does it care about everyone's past. The concern is how to help everyone recover. The rehabilitation program emphasizes the abstinence of all drugs, and has only one requirement for its members: they want to give up drugs. NA suggests that every member should be open-minded and self-adjusting. Members do not need to pay dues, do not need to swear, membership is not affected by age, gender, race, religious belief, come and go freely.

On the other hand, NA lacks a strict organization, and its existence and activity are anonymous. So far, there is no scientific evaluation on the effectiveness of NA (such as long-term integrity rate). Moreover, due to the differences in the structure and activities of various organizations, it is more difficult to evaluate scientifically.

Social work in community drug treatment service in China

Since the implementation of the anti-drug law of the People's Republic of China, the basic status of community drug treatment (rehabilitation) has been established in the new drug treatment system in China. At present, the effective implementation rate of community drug treatment (rehabilitation) is low and the relapse rate is high. From the perspective of drug users, it is found that the frequent relapse of drug users is due to the combined effect of personal, family and social factors, while their willingness to quit is affected by four factors: the frequency of social workers' help and education, the times of detoxification, the relationship between family members and interpersonal communication (the proportion of drug users).

Social workers can use case management method, family social work method, group social work method, and community social work method to intervene community drug users. Family social work primarily provides family services to improve parent-child or husband-wife relationships. Group social work specifically includes NA self-help groups, employment and school support groups, peer education groups (peer education), and other types. In practice, different strategies are frequently organically blended to build an integrated drug recovery social work method.

Case management

(1) Identify subject and build professional relationships
    a.   Discover service subject
    b.   Sign service agreement and set up files
(2) Basic and psychosocial information collection
    a.   Basic information of subject
    b.   Collection of psychosocial data
(3) Subject needs analysis and planning
    a.   Social ecosystem analysis of service subject
    b.   Problems and demands of service subject
    c.   Identify service objectives
    d.   Development of service plan
(4) Implementation of service plan
    a.   Emotional counseling of service subject
    b.   Link resources for service subject
    c.   Improving family relations
    d.   Strengthen the motivation and desire for detoxification
    e.   Establishing social support network
(5) Assessment and closure
    a.   Evaluation of results
    b.   Process assessment
    c.   Close the case and follow up the service

Family Social Work

1. Stage I: The social worker meets the aid's family member for the first time, assesses the aid's needs, and creates a preliminary trust and collaboration connection with the family member who loves him dearly.
2. Stage II: Create a stable cooperative connection with the assistance's family members, conduct a full evaluation of the assistance's family members' problems, and specify the service intervention's aims and basic requirements.
3. Stage III: Define professional roles, apply professional skills to persuade family members to seek help, and aid family members in resolving difficulties.
4. Stage IV: Negotiate the conclusion of the service with the assistance's family members, and describe and integrate the full service activity's progress.

Group work

(1) Preparation stage
    a.   Recruitment
    b.   Set group goals
    c.   Write a group plan
    d.   Collaborate on resources such as event sites, funding, and so forth.
(2) Initial stage
    a.   Team members get to know one another
    b.   Create group requirements
    c.   Create a positive group culture
    d.   Internalization objectives
(3) Stage of mid-term consolidation
    a.   Consolidate the general goal
    b.   Conflict resolution and coordination
    c.   Get rid of defensive thinking
(4) Late turning stage
    a.   Maintain a positive group atmosphere.
    b.   Bring together members of a team to pursue a common purpose
    c.   Provide resources
    d.   Provide a link to information
(5) End stage

   a.   Deal with parting emotions
   b.   Consolidate previous experience
   c.   Summary of group evaluation

Self-help group

1. Understand the past experience, current mentality and practical difficulties of the subjects, and enhance mutual understanding between social workers and drug users
2. Change subjects' bad self-role cognition, recognize and reflect on themselves, remove labels and regain self-confidence
3. Let care be taken into the families of drug users, and guide group members and their families to understand and support each other
4. Invite the successful team members to introduce their experience and help, explore the potential and resources within the team, and benefit all team members
5. Cooperate with drug treatment publicity activities, play psychodrama with drug users as the protagonist, improve the concept of making friends, rebuild social network and enrich healthy social activities

Family support group

1. Through the mutual introduction between social workers and members, promote the understanding between group members and the understanding of the group, and enhance the sense of trust among members through ice breaking games
2. Social workers popularize the knowledge about drugs and detoxification to the family members of drug users in the community, and promote the understanding of the family members of drug users in the community by watching relevant detoxification videos
3. Family members of community drug users discuss and summarize the skills and methods of communication with community drug users. Social workers analyze and teach the skills of communication with community drug users
4. After the previous group activities, discuss what problems still exist in getting along with community drug users, and work out solutions together, share experiences, and summarize by social workers

5. Social workers help team members to consolidate the skills they have learned before. Team members share their gains in the group and end the group

Employment support group

1. Through the mutual introduction between social workers and community drug users, promote the mutual understanding and understanding of the group among community drug users. Through ice breaking games, break the gap between group members, and enhance the sense of trust among group members
2. Social workers play videos to community drug users about their successful finding jobs, so that they can understand that community drug users can find jobs, and enhance the self-confidence of community drug users through group games
3. The social workers summarize and share the employment skills, and provide guidance according to the situation of each group member, so as to promote the community drug users to master certain employment skills
4. Hold a mock interview recruitment fair, social workers as interviewers, conduct simulated interviews for community drug users, and then discuss the advantages and disadvantages of drug users in each community through group members, and summarize the interview experience
5. The social workers help the community drug users to consolidate the employment skills they have learned before. The group members share their gains in the group and end the group

Peer Education Group

1. The social worker introduces himself, facilitates the formation of a group contract, and promotes the formation of relationships through ice-breaker games. The peer counselor explains about his drug rehabilitation experience and expresses his experiences in groups with the theme "Farewell to Yesterday."
2. The activity's theme, "feeling," is introduced through a game, and participants are encouraged to discuss the impact of emotions. The peer counselor discusses the impact of negative emotions on drug rehabilita-

tion and his or her experience with emotion regulation, and the group members discuss and synthesize the information.

3. Encourage group members to discuss how to foster self-confidence by having peers describe their own journey of becoming a peer counselor, and how to enhance self-efficacy in helping others.

4. Use the game to elicit the activity's topic, "life," and to urge the team members to think about and cherish life. Share the changes in life before and after detoxification with the partner counselor.

5. The social worker leads the group members in a review of the activity's content, the group members discuss their personal gains, the peer counselor shares the group members' growth as a result of their participation in the group, and the social worker delivers a final summary.

Community care

Those with moderate or severe intolerable withdrawal symptoms	To guide oral methadone maintenance treatment, supplemented by psychotherapy and environmental intervention. The minimum living allowance recipients can apply for exemption of methadone taking fee. The mild patients were mainly intervened by psychotherapy, environmental intervention, employment recommendation and healthy lifestyle
Patients with anxiety and depression	Psychological treatment can be given through case consultation, peer influence, group treatment or drug treatment by specialist
Those who have just come out of the Institute and have no financial resources, serious illness or family financial difficulties	Open the green channel of street emergency rescue, provide temporary subsidy of 200–500 yuan through the street civil affairs department to tide over the crisis temporarily, and then seek the support of family members or relatives. At the same time, organize the social security department through the network to deal with the minimum living allowance for those who meet the conditions, and recommend work to those who have higher work intention
Those who have no job but strong desire to work	After the employment guidance intervention, the Ministry of labor and social security and relatives and friends resources help to solve the employment problem

Without work and less willing to work	Do not introduce employment for the time being, first through psychotherapy guidance to improve their willingness to work; the willingness to work is 1–10 points, the urgent need to work is 10 points, unwilling to work is 1 point, when the willingness to work reaches about 7 points, there is a strong demand for work, do pre-employment counseling, recommend employment
Patients with physical diseases	According to the needs, the community doctors can provide health consultation and treatment. The treatment expenses can be paid by themselves or their family members, relatives and friends. According to the policy, the destitute people can apply to the civil affairs department for certain subsidies, and can also be solved through various channels such as medical insurance
Poor family cohesion and adaptability	Through social workers to communicate with their families, family therapy can be carried out to change their cognition and promote the improvement of their family relationship
Lack of social support system	To help establish social support system, all members of the community rehabilitation guidance room should do a good job in providing, listening, counseling and caring, actively help to solve some practical difficulties and problems, obtain the recognition and trust of the subject, become a part of his social support system, and explore and develop the support system for family members and relatives. Eliminate their loneliness and helplessness, no one to talk to, no one to discuss and help, self abandonment and other phenomena

References

Du, X. (2002). Therapeutic community and its practice in compulsory detoxification settings. *CHINESE JOURNAL OF DRUG DEPENDENCE*, *11*(4), 310-312. https://doi.org/10.3969/j.issn.1007-9718.2002.04.019

Fan, Z. (2005). Structuring of "Working Mode in Transitional Society" – Experiences from Drugs Banning in Shanghai and Reflection of It. *JOURNAL OF SOCIAL SCIENCES*(6), 72–78. https://doi.org/10.3969/j.issn.0257-5833.2005.06.013

Fan, Z. (2009). Social work practice of drug treatment. In C. S. W. Association (Ed.), *REPORTS ON DEVELOPMENT OF SOCIAL WORK IN CHINA （1988–2008）* (pp. 196–208).

Fan, Z., & Lv, W. (2005). Experience of and self-examination on Shanghai social work for drug control. *CHINESE JOURNAL OF DRUG DEPENDENCE, 14*(5), 388–391. https://doi.org/10.3969/j.issn.1007-9718.2005.05.017

Fan, Z., Lv, W., & Yu, J. (2008). Preliminary exploration of community drug rehabilitation model – Taking Shanghai drug control social work as an example. *CHINESE JOURNAL OF DRUG DEPENDENCE, 18*(2), 152–154.

Fang, W. (2006). Analysis of drug abuse and social policy among young people in Hong Kong. *YOUTU STUDIES, 1*, 16–21. https://doi.org/CNKI:SUN:QLTS. 0.2006-01-003

Li, X. (2012). Consideration on the Construction of Drug Control Social Work in Yunnan Police Official Academy. *Journal of Yuannan Police Officer Academy*(5), 50–53. https://doi.org/10.3969/j.issn.1672-6057.2012.05.011

Mai Yumin.Wang Gaoxi: New Era, New Mission, New Journey——The "Guangdong Model" of Lianzhong Anti-drug Social Workers is a Model for National Output[J].The Big Society,2019(Z1):65–69.

Chu Chenge.Thirty years of research on Chinese anti-drug law from the perspective of discipline[J].Chinese Social Science Evaluation,2020(01):118–129+159–160.

Lai Yuzhen. Optimize resource allocation and improve voluntary drug rehabilitation[N]. China Anti-drug News, 2020–10–16(006).

Li, X., & Ma, R. (2014). The development history and practical operation mode of social work for drug treatment in China. *Journal of Guangdong University of Technology*(*Social Sciences Edition*), *14*(6), 5–10. https://doi.org/10.3969/j.issn.1671-623X.2014.06.001

Li, X., Yin, W., Zhao, J., Chen, M., Jiang, Z., & Wang, W. (2018). Establishment of community drug treatment and community rehabilitation mechanism based on cloud data. *Popular Science*(4), 14–16.

Service, C. o. S. Z. S. (2003). http://www.cszqss.org/.

Service, C. o. S. Z. S. (2007). http://www.pdswa.org/.

Tang, D. (2008). Implementation of anti drug law: good law calls for social workers. *China Society Daily*, 1–2.

Tang, X., & Huang, X. (2008). The role of social workers in different modes of detoxification. *CHINA SOCIETY PERIODICAL*(27), 26–28.

Yang, M., Feng, Y., Zhang, G., Guo, J., Wu, T., Huang, P., & Li, J. (2002). Rehabilitation model of China-U.S.A Daytop Village on drug detoxification. *SOFT SCIENCE OF HEALTH, 16*(5), 23–26. https://doi.org/10.3969/j.issn.1003-2800.2002.05.009

Yang, X. (2005). *Community drug control under the intervention of professional social workers in Shanghai* East China University of Science and Technology].

Zhang, M. (2011). *Community detoxification and social support.* Suzhou University Press.

Zhang, Y., & Wang, Y. (2014). A review of the historical evolution of China's anti drug social work. *CHINESE JOURNAL OF DRUG DEPENDENCE, 23*(2), 156–160.

Zhao, M., Zhang, R., & Wang, G. (2011). *Foundation of social work for drug treatment.* Military Medical Science Press.

Zhong, Y. (2010). *Exploration on social work of community drug rehabilitation from the perspective of system reform* Zhongshan University].

PART II

Developments in the medication-assisted treatment for opioid users in Central Asia and China: Barriers and facilitators

Ingo Ilja Michels and Heino Stöver

Abstract

The development of medication-based treatment (MAT) of opioid dependence in Central Asia and the PR of China has only been treated marginally in the international specialist literature in recent years, although it is precisely in these two regions that it can be exemplified which supporting and which obstructing factors play a role. The professional world is usually more interested in the development of MAT in the USA, Canada, Australia or in Europe. Why Central Asia and China? There are several reasons for this: Central Asia is marked to a considerable extent by increasing "trade" (via smuggling, clandestine sale and money laundering) and consumption of opiates and opioids (especially heroin). On the basis of a systematic literature review and expert interviews, this article explores the barriers and facilitators in provision of MAT in Kazakhstan, Kyrgyzstan, and the People's Republic of China. To review the dynamics since 2011, we conducted a systematic literature review including national statistical data and grey literature to complement the additional expert interviews. The results indicate that there is strong evidence that medication-assisted treatment (MAT) is effective in enabling people to reduce or cease injecting drug use, greatly reducing the risk of blood-borne viruses such as HIV. The implications of this study suggest a need for future research to design better methods for successful scaling-up of access and integration of MAT for opioid users.

Keywords: Central Asia, China, treatment of opioid dependence, medication-assisted treatment, methadone, opioid use

Introduction

Medication-assisted treatment, which is also known as methadone maintenance treatment, opioid-substitution treatment or opioid-agonist therapy, is a medically and psycho-socially supported intervention for people suffering from negative health consequences of habitual opioid use. These treatment methods have shown to decrease morbidity, mortality, enhance the retention in treatment, and reduce opioid use (Hedrich et al., 2008; Latypov et al., 2010; Mattick et al., 2009). Evidence shows that medication-assisted treatment (MAT) is also effective in reducing the risk of blood-borne viruses such as HIV and Hepatitis C among people who inject drugs (MacArthur et al., 2012). MAT has shown wider health, economic, psychological and social benefits. With its core aims being to reduce or cease illicit opioid use, prevent future harms associated with opioid use, and improve quality of life and well-being, MAT is a vital public health and harm-reduction intervention (WHO, 2009). According to the recommendations of the World Health Organization (WHO) and the United Nations Office on drugs and Crime (UNODC), MAT should be provided as part of a comprehensive package for the prevention, treatment and care for people who inject drugs and live with HIV/AIDS. The package should also envisage additional interventions, such as needle and syringe programs (NSPs), HIV testing and counselling, antiretroviral therapy, targeted information, education and communication for people who inject drugs, and their sexual partners as well as vaccination, diagnosis and treatment of viral hepatitis and tuberculosis. These interventions work best if access to MAT is available, user-friendly, and supported not only by medical staff, but also by local communities and specialization programs including accreditation of physicians, competence-enhancement trainings, and collaboration with local law enforcement agencies (WHO 2009).

MAT is often provided within a long-term outpatient treatment service alongside psycho-social therapy to aid in navigating daily life and functionality, without furthering negative consequences of opioid dependency (Sordo et al., 2017; World Health Organization, 2014). MAT is also a preferred term as it avoids suggesting that opioid use should be substituted or maintained (NIDA, 2021) and offers a more neutral understanding of drug treatment that includes other types of medications besides methadone (e.g. codeine, suboxone/buprenorphine/naloxone).

In this article, we review how these goals have been achieved within the challenging conditions of Kazakhstan, Kyrgyzstan[1] and PR China where MAT had been or is still treated with caution. The international positive experiences that foreground public health through harm-reduction and human rights approaches, encourage local governments to implement

---

1 The inclusion of Tajikistan in this contribution could not be implemented. In this regard, reference is made to the article by Michels et.al.2021

MAT in order to reduce overdose rates and rising of infectious diseases (Csete, 2016; HRI, 2014). However, the most recent evidence shows that funding of MAT in low and middle-income countries has been visibly decreasing, leaving Central Asia and Eastern Europe with less than 27 % of international donorship (Serebryakova et al., 2021). In both Central Asia and PR China, the official numbers of registered people who use opioids and the estimated grey numbers differ vastly (Zabransky et al., 2014)(Zhao 2019). In Central Asia, approximately only 2,500 of around 400,000 opioid dependent people are on treatment with opioid agonists (mostly methadone). In Kyrgyzstan this number is 1,450 and in Kazakhstan 353 (Michels, 2021). Although there is MAT in prisons in Kyrgyzstan, access to treatment is inconsistent (Azbel, 2017). Experts argue that MAT could play an essential role in the public health reforms in Central Asia and China, if the existing opposition from the local governments recedes (Michels, 2021). These developments suggest a need for a more in-depth understanding of how various factors – facilitators and barriers – could explain the intermittent and fluctuating provision of MAT in the two regions.

In general, facilitators of MAT are defined through: 1) *availability* (provision, medications), 2) *accessibility* (range of providers, opening hours, geographical coverage), 3) *affordability* (reimbursement schemes), and 4) *acceptability* (stigma, stakeholders' perception of MAT) (EMCDDA, 2021). In turn, barriers to MAT are understood as mediated by local and national legal frameworks, policies, drug use prevalence and types of drugs, treatment quality control, as well as overall socio-economic situation (EMCDDA, 2021). In combination, both facilitators and barriers can also be categorized as institutional, programmatic, attitudinal, and systematic (Grella, 2020). In this article, we aim to qualitatively analyze the complexity of these factors across all latter four dimensions by mapping out the changes of the past decade through the published empirical evidence.

Background

The Central Asian (CA) countries Kazakhstan, the Kyrgyz Republic, Tajikistan, Turkmenistan, and Uzbekistan – include more than 60 million ethnically, culturally, and religiously diverse people distributed over a geographical area twice the size of continental Europe, getting independent when the Soviet Union dissolved in 1991. (Central Asia Human Development Report: Bringing Down Barriers) (CADAP 2020) Since independence, they have faced huge challenges such as inappropriate and unaffordable health systems. Many different groups have a role to play: national politicians and local governments, the health professions, the scientific community, the private sector and civil society organizations, as well as the global health community. Today, Central Asia (CA) has become a key region for the international activities tackling illegal drugs and related problems – specifically the problems with illicit opioids, and increasingly, also cannabinoids. Drugs and drug related problems, such as crimes, dependency or infectious diseases (such as HIV/AIDS, hepatitis, and TB) are key challenges for the international community and each state. (Jolley, 2012) (Latypov, 2014) (Zabransky, 2014) (Michels, 2017) The European Union has supported the CA countries' for several years to support a balanced drug policy in line with the EU Drug Strategy 2013–2020, EU Drug Strategy 2021–2030 and the EU Central Asia Drug Action Plan 2014–2020 (EU Drug Strategies). According to the annual reports of the drug situation in 2012 and 2013 and recently 2018 (Regional Report on the Drug Situation in Central Asia, 2019) there are first signs of a reduction of drug dependency and infectious diseases (at least of the officially registered persons with drug dependence or infectious diseases such as HIV/AIDS and Hepatitis C). It is difficult to analyse the reasons for this trend, but it can be stabilized by a common initiative of CA countries to tackle these drug related problems on a regional level. All countries in Central Asia are supporting the common view of the UN bodies (UN Drug Convention 1961, Art. 38; and Political Declaration 2009) to implement all practicable measures for *"prevention, early identification; treatment, education, after-care and rehabilitation and social reintegration"* of drug dependent people and the UNGASS outcome document from 2016 (UNGASS 2016).

The same is true for the PR China. The number of registered drug users increased from 70,000 in 1990 to more than 2,8 mio. by the end of 2018. One major drug-related problem has been the spread of HIV. Figures from the Chinese Center for Disease Control and Prevention, World Health Organization, and UNAIDS estimate that there were 1.25 million people living with HIV/AIDS in China at the end of 2018, with 135,000 new infections from 2017 (Michels, 2007)(Zhang 2019)(Zhao, 2020. The reported incidence of HIV/AIDS in China is relatively low. About 50 % of them are injecting drug users, but sexual transmission gradually began to overtake the originally predominant routes of transmission. Since 2003, China has implemented harm-reduction measures such as needle-and-syringe programmes and methadone maintenance treatment for controlling the spread of HIV/AIDS. Although compulsory treatment options are still mostly used, voluntary treatment facilities are growing rapidly, and psychotherapeutic treatment options are being implemented. Also in China we recognize

„*still a large number of drug users (…) although the growth rate has slowed down. The major abused drugs are methamphetamine, heroin and ke-tamine. The abuse of synthetic drugs such as methamphetamine continues to increase, with 80 % of newly discovered users abusing synthetic drugs. Among traditional drugs, heroin abuse increase is slowing*". (Zhao, 2020)

In both, Central Asian countries as well as in the PR China modern methods of treatment of drug use disorders, according to the UNODC/WHO International Standards of treatment of drug use disorders (International Standards, 2020) have been implemented, including Medication Assisted Treatment (MAT), although the provision of treatment is limited and not affordable for all those in need and psycho-social assistance is still widely not available. Especially social work is missing or still in an infancy phase.

Drug addiction is still seen in both Central Asia and the People's Republic of China more as a "social deviation" problem than as a treatable disease; repressive drug laws mean that many of those affected have to face long prison terms and that the police and judiciary are not cooperating well with health services. This and the registration system promote the social exclusion of those affected.

Key indicators per country

MAT in PR China

A comprehensive overview on the development of MAT in PR China gave Marienfelda et.al. already in 2015 (Marienfelda, 2015) and Lee together with Newman, including the longterm experiences from Hong Kong (Lee 2017) and earlier (2010) by Yin et.al.(Yin, 2010).(also: Sun 2015)

Problems with opiate use, injection drug use (IDU), and transmission of human immunodeficiency virus (HIV) are closely interrelated in China, which has an estimated 780,000 HIV infected individuals and over 2 million registered drug users (Lu, 2008) (Meise, 2009). Injection of drugs is associated with 42 % of HIV transmissions, and about 45 % of people who inject drugs in China are estimated to share needles and injection equipment (Shen, 2005) (Lu, 2008). To address these problems, China has undertaken major initiatives over the past decade, including introduction and scale-up of methadone maintenance treatment (MMT) (Sullivan, 2007). The early success of small pilot MMT programs introduced in 2004 (Yin, 2010) has been followed by rapid expansion of MMT programs that follow standardized clinical protocols (Zhang 2018), and physicians providing

MMT participate in a structured, centrally-run, national training. By the end of 2019, more than 160,000 patients had been enrolled in more than 730 clinics established since 2005, but with a decrease in the lat years. Earlier studies evaluating implementation and scale up of MMT programs across China reported use of lower than generally recommended dosages of methadone, misconceptions about MMT and high drop-out rates (Chen, 2019).

This overview of Marienfelda et.al. explained well the developmet of MAT in China as well as historically it has been developed with support from Hong Kong which started more than 40 years ago with MAT, according to the British model. The latest overview is given by Tianzhen Chen and Min Zhao in 2019 (Chen, 2019). *China* kicked off a methadone maintenance program as the main component of the harm reduction strategies starting from 2003. The first eight MAT clinics in the country were set up in five provinces during the pilot phase from March to June 2004. After showing positive results, MAT has become an important aspect of the rehabilitation of people who used opioids. By the end of 2016, a total of 773 MAT clinics had been set up in 29 out of 34 provinces of China including 24 mobile clinics, to improve access for the rural population with around 160,000 clients of an estimated 1.5 million heroin users (see Lee & Newman, 2017). However, certain restrictions applied to the provision of MAT have led to inconsistent results discussed below. According to unofficial statistics, at least 10 million people are believed to use drugs in China, of which 1,3 million are opioid users (HRI, 2014). However, restrictions applied to the provision of MAT have led to inconsistent results that is evidenced in individual country profiles.

The scale of the MAT distribution and drug treatment policy differs drastically. Within 13 years after commencing the methadone treatment in 2003, the Chinese government authorized the opening of 773 MAT clinics in 29 provinces of the country (Chen & Zhao, 2019), that provide both methadone and buprenorphine in the program (Harm Reduction International, 2014). *China* has made significant progress towards implementing and enhancing harm reduction programs in recent years. The country has launched a treatment with methadone and was scheduled to serve more than 160,000 heroin users by the end of the 2018; there are similar ambitions for increasing the availability needle and syringe programs around the country ad to increase the number of voluntary counselling and testing (VCT) sites, especially in high prevalence areas and have explored interventions that increase the uptake of VCT among people who use drugs; and the role of the NGOs is an emerging, though underused, means to provide HIV-related outreach services among this marginalized group. In such a large country there are many barriers to overcome before complete implementation of a comprehensive and far-reaching harm reduction strategy. China is well on its way towards achieving its goals (Chen & Zhao, 2019; Sullivan et al., 2014).

MAT in Central Asia

Central Asia is among the top regions for high opiate consumption marking 0,9 % of the population (UNODC, 2020). The region also has the highest numbers for injection drug use in carceral settings reporting one in five people who had injected a drug at least once during the imprisonment (UNODC 2020).

The development and implementation of MAT in *Central Asia* has been stagnating in the past few years. The implementation is accompanied by strong media and other public campaigns against this type of drug treatment and harm reduction measures, which had been claiming that MAT will lead to a "new type of addiction", that people who use drugs are "poisoned with a dangerous drug" referring to methadone, or that this treatment intervention is another form of "Western imperialism" etc. Against this background, the local governments and Ministries of Health and Internal Affairs have been very cautious in implementing MAT reflecting the skepticism that is still dominating Central Asian drug policy landscape. We believe that this opposition widely communicates the influence from Russia against MAT, too (Golichenko, 2020; Michels et al., 2021; Pape & Pape, 2019).

Despite the above cited challenges, implementation of MAT has undergone several successful stages even if small in scale. In the early 2010's we saw an increase in access to opioid substitution treatment in *Kazakhstan* (World Health Organization, 2012) with methadone as the only medication prescribed in MAT programs since 2015. The medication is distributed to healthcare institutions and costs less than one US Dollar (informburo.kz, 2017) per a single dose, whereas the heroin in the black-market costs around 23 US Dollars. As of December 31 2019, there were 296 people in treatment, which is only 0.3 % of the estimated 94,600 people who use opioid drugs (Abishev, 2020), including 235 men and 61 women. As of July 7, 2021, 326 people were enrolled in the program, 117 of whom were HIV patients (azattyq.org, 2021). For 2019, 44 people were enrolled in the program. However, evidence shows that strong anti-MAT propaganda in Kazakhstan is among the main barriers to scaling-up of the treatment, often misinformation making a louder argument rather than evidence of the positive effects from treatment implementation (Parsons et al., 2014).

Current situation in Kazakhstan

The Kazakh program did not yet succeeded in expanding the program, because with the number of patients reached so far, around 4 % of the officially registered opioid dependents in Kazakhstan, it will of course hardly be possible to achieve the ambitious goals of reducing the number of opioid users or to reduce infections with HIV and hepatitis C, which are quite high at 38 % and over 60 %, respectively. In Germany we succeeded in reducing the HIV infections among injecting drug users to less than 4 % with the expansion of infection prevention measures such as syringes exchange and opioid agonist treatment, but we had to fight hard for this togeher with self-help organizations such as the AIDS help and drug counseling centers, supported by the Ministry of Health with state funds for education. And doctors had to be found and trained to offer this treatment, as well as social workers to support the clients. There are now over 80,000 opiopid users under treatment, over 40 % of the estimated total. And it has been possible that this treatment is recognized and supported not only in the professional world, but also in society as a whole, and also by politics! There were also decisive changes in the allocation modalities: In Germany, too, an HIV or hepatitis C infection or pregnancy in drug-addicted women as well as long-term opioid dependence and a minimum age were initially a prerequisite for entry into the program. These hurdles have now been removed: the *diagnosis of opioid addiction* is now sufficient as an entry criterion for treatment to take place. The treatment costs are covered by the health insurance. That was an important step, against a lot of resistance. It is also a treatment in a multidisciplinary team of medical doctors, psychologists, social workers and members of self-help groups. This is important in order to achieve long-term goals and a stabilization of the mental and physical health of the patient. Achieving stable – and for those affected – contented abstinence or at least reducing the consumption of opioids and other psychoactive substances is still the aim of the treatment, but not its prerequisite.

In contrast, the number of treatments is still the highest in Pavlodar, but with 78 patients it is still quite low regarding the estimated high number of opioid users in this region. Nevertheless, the employees there are highly motivated and very committed and they were pioneers in treatment! In Kazakhstan there are predominantly committed women who work as doctors, nurses and social workers in this area and committed representatives of non-governmental organizations (NGOs), especially former drug addicts, who do tireless and mostly voluntary work here. It is also gratifying that 96 % of HIV positive patients are in ART treatment. But there is still no treatment option for HCV patients, althgough with the new drugs a hepatitis C infection can be cured, even if the treatment costs are still very high.(Nadezhda Cherchenko 2021)(Michels, 2021)

Current situation in the Kyrgyz Republic

With some differences in the scale of the implementation, similar situation is observed in *Kyrgyzstan*. The MAT had been implemented quite early in the country beginning in 2002 and has been part of the comprehensive treatment options for opioid users in the country, including detoxification (permanently and on an outpatient basis); short-term detoxification analogues of MAT for people dependent on opioid use; outpatient rehabilitation; complex provision of services with TB and HIV infections ("Single Window Model"). Today, there are 24 MAT sites in the country out of which 15 are within the healthcare organizations and 9 are incorporated in the penal system. There are still difficulties: Restrictions in access and possibility of receiving legal aid for patients (Michels, 2021).

A comprehensive overview on MAT development in Kyrgyzstan was developed by an overview from Zhyldyz Bakirova gfrom the Republican Narcological Centre in Bishkek:

"When processing the data on *"The main indicators of MTM for current patients in the republic from 01.01.2017 until 09.06.2021"* it was found that at the beginning of 01.2021 the MAT consisted of 1190 people (including 96 women) for the period from 01.01.2017. Until 09.06.2021, 2115 people (including 141 women) with opium addiction passed. 1,114 patients dropped out of the program during the reporting period, of which 21.4 % died after death. 1,437 patients were admitted to the program during the reporting period, of which 34.2 % were initially taken. At the end of the reporting period, 871 patients take part in the MAT, of which 50 % are persons aged 30 to 44, 42 % do not work, 53 % have secondary education, 58 % are not married or divorced. 8.7 % of patients receiving MAT got a job, 646 people were tested for HIV infection during the reporting period, of which 4.9 % were HIV-positive, 647 patients who have been on MAT for 6 months or more have been tested for HIV, of which 35.7 % are persons with a confirmed diagnosis of HIV who are registered with the AIDS service and receive antiretroviral therapy. 548 patients who are still on MAT for 12 months or more, and who underwent instrumental examination (X-ray / fluorography) for TB at the end of the reporting period, of which 11.1 % with a confirmed TB diagnosis and receiving anti-TB treatment." (Bakirova, 2021)(Michels, 2021)

Methods

Following the slow progress in the adaptation and only a partial implementation of MAT in both regions, our purpose was to raise a number of possible research directions and provide a synthesis of the available data. This presents with several limitations and challenges. For example, in China, data specifying the exact numbers and treatment methods, including the way of ways of acquiring statistical figures are generally a classified information[2]. Usually, publicly available data comes from international organizations such as the Global Fund, WHO, and UNODC who carry out annual monitoring. Similarly, national statistical reports from Central Asia have been reported to carry falsifications of numbers as well as poor data management leading to unreliable information (Boltaev et al., 2012; Zabransky et al., 2014). In this paper, we reviewed the literature in accordance to its relevance, research type (original empirical research or review), and methods. To address the gaps in obtaining the relevant data and insider knowledge, we used both systematic literature review and qualitative expert interview methods as the basis for our analysis.

Expert interviews were conducted in two forms: written communication and via video-chat platforms (e.g. Skype / Zoom) through June to September of 2021. All interviews were structured as the experts were given six open-end questions to elaborate on the local situation on the MAT provision. We interviewed a total of five experts: three from Kazakhstan and one for each Kyrgyzstan and China. All experts solicited data from local governments, NGOs, and media, and provided written technical reviews of the available grey literature in their local languages.

The search strategy for the systematic review involved an initial broad search on the Web of Science, PubMed, and Google Scholar databases to retrieve peer-reviewed research and review articles published in English between 2011 and 2021. The initial search also helped to identify

---

2 Personal communication with a research associate in drug treatment program at Shanghai Mental Health Center and with Kazakh and Kyrgyz experts. The research associate had been Aysel Sultan, former employee of the SOLID project

relevant, supporting grey literature including international reports, local government reports, national epidemiological statistics, and NGO reports. Keywords searched between February and April 2021. The initial search on the Web of Science and PubMed revealed 6,019 results for the following key terms "opioid substitution treatment OR opioid agonist therapy OR methadone maintenance treatment OR medication-assisted treatment". A refined search in both databases yielded a total of 528 articles mentioning China and 69 mentioning Central Asia. Results for China were used in the similar combination and order, but further filtered with 'addiction' OR 'opioid use' OR 'harm reduction'. All initial results were then further refined with categories of 'research article', 'legislation', 'practice guidelines' and then filtered according to full-text availability. After the duplicates were removed and the search was refined to include only publications on MAT for opioid use, a total of 47 publications were included in the study.

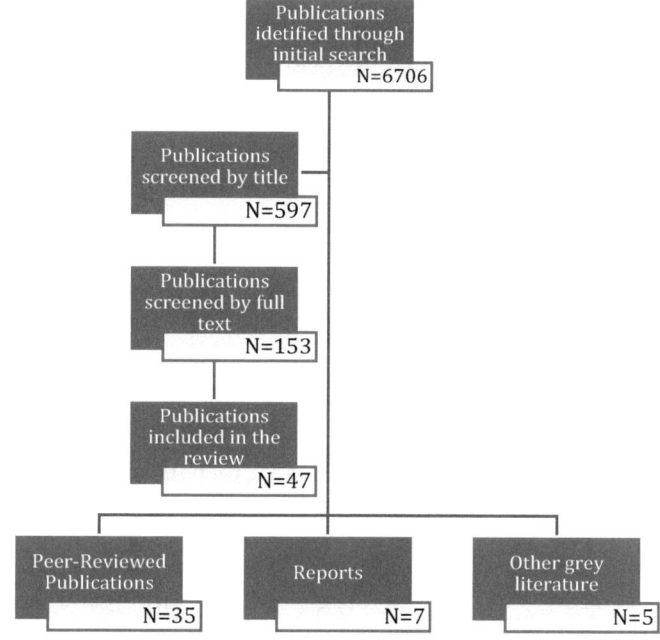

Figure 1. Flow chart of the literature selection criteria

In the final selection, we included studies that directly examined the effects of MAT on long-term opioid use in five countries. Search results have been categorized according to the following themes: (a) study duration; (b) data collection methods and sample size; (c) participants – population cohort; (d) treatment – MAT involving methadone, buprenorphine, codeine, and morphine; and finally, (e) policy indicators and harm-reduction. We then analyzed the selected articles on the basis of the following six questions: *1.* What development and changes are visible in the demographics of MAT enrolment in the last ten years?; *2.* How are the MAT services structured in terms of provision, referral of patients, facilitation of access, prescription, and the actual progress of the treatment (the probing questions included the number and the kind of local staff such as narcologists/medical doctors, nurses, social workers, activists engaged in MAT services)?; *3.* Why in most sites, methadone is the only prescribed agonist?; *4.* What were the reasons for the decrease in the number of patients?; *5.* What impact did law enforcement, medical considerations, general political climate and other, external factors have with regard to the development of MAT programs?; *6.* Which role have NGOs played with respect to psycho-social support for MAT patients? In the following section, we present our analysis of the literature divided into six sub-sections in response to these questions.

Results: Identifying barriers and facilitators

The results of the literature review have shown that there is scarcity of studies and available empirical knowledge on the development of MAT programs in Central Asia more than in China. While the provision of MAT in Central Asia is mostly based on short-term internationally sponsored programs, China has adapted ongoing national strategies. Studies included in this review have looked at MAT implementation both within the context of prevalence prevention (e.g. prisons, HIV/AIDS prevention) as well as drug treatment programs (e.g. methadone-maintenance treatment). However, these were the majority of studies where MAT programs were not the sole focus of the studies, rather one element of a comprehensive treatment. We then narrowed the studies down to only those which reviewed the efficiency of MAT program in drug treatment settings and that measured the above listed six criteria.

1. What are the developments in the demographics of MAT enrolment in the last ten years Kazakhstan, Kyrgyzstan, and PR China?

The development with MAT clinics and medications in Central Asia offers varied policy implications. Per our expert interviews, there are 24 MAT sites in the *Kyrgyzstan* as of January 2021. The sites are supported by the Global Fund (GFATM), Center for Disease Control (CDC) and with only minimal involvement of the Ministry of Health. As a rule, these sites are located in family medical centers at the primary healthcare level, in medical institutions that provide treatment services for HIV/AIDS and tuberculosis, or in correctional facilities. All MAT sites report basic data on the number of patients registered as people who inject drugs or as diagnosed with addiction. According to the standards and the staff list of these MAT sites, each site has a capacity for approximate 50 patients and includes a doctor (narcologist, psychiatrist), a nurse, a psychologist/psychotherapist, a social worker, and a cleaner. Experts report these sites to be generally understaffed with nurses oftentimes performing the function of a social worker, which invariably reduces the quality of social work provision. Patients are admitted for MAT treatment according to following algorithm: 1) Determining if the individual meets admission criteria: *a)* if there is an opioid dependence syndrome and *b)* confirmation of injection of illicit opioids and active opioid use at the time of referral; 2) Determining the presence of contraindications: *a)* ensure that the patient is informed and counselled about the MAT, *b)* obtain informed consent for treatment; 3) Introducing the patient at the Special Advisory Committee (SAC) meeting and obtaining approval from the SAC to admit the patient to the maintenance therapy program; 4) Signing a contract between the patient and the supportive care provider; 5) Entering the patient data on the national narcological registry: *a)* recording patient's medical history as part of the program

In Kyrgyzstan, the recent state report on the "Main indicators of MAT for current patients by the state from January 2017 until June 2021" found that at the beginning of the year 2021, there were a total of 1,190 patients, including 96 women, enrolled in the local MAT programs. 1,114 patients dropped out of the program during the reporting period, 21.4 % of them by death. 1,437 patients were enrolled in the program during the reporting period, of whom 34.2 % were primary enrollees. At the end of the reporting period, 871 patients were enrolled in MAT, of whom 50 % were between the ages of 30 and 44, 42 % were unemployed, 53 % had high school education, and 58 % were single or divorced.

2. *How are the MAT services structured in terms of provision, referral of patients, facilitation of access, prescription, and the actual progress of the treatment?*

Retention rates in MAT are often treated as the main measure of treatment outcome. In China, the enhancement of retention rates is pursued through optimization and diversification of treatment by targeting innovative counselling models and digitization of monitoring systems (see Marienfeld et al., 2017). In the example of Shanghai Municipal Centre for Disease Control and Prevention, a recent study on outcome measures have reported only 25 % retention in MAT (see Zhang et al., 2019). Some indicators such as reduction of infectious diseases or opioid use depend on the specific circumstances despite the presence of MAT programs. In addition, more barriers and less facilitators, which suggests that further research is needed to study more efficient scaling-up methods in both regions. The implementation and successful MAT coverage of the vulnerable populations are highly dependent on the local conditions and national policies (WHO, 2014). Previous studies focusing on Central Asia have uncovered a number of difficulties in the provision of MAT, citing systemic, socio-economic, political and societal opposition among other factors (LaMonaca et al., 2019; Latypov, 2010; Parsons et al., 2014).

3. *Why in most sites, methadone is the only prescribed agonist?*

Methadone is the only agonist medication approved in China despite the ongoing trials testing the effectiveness of buprenorphine/naloxone for opioid users (Dong et al., 2019; Lucas et al., 2012). According to our expert interview, while methadone is the most widely used medication in MAT program, there are some exceptions, like the Shanghai Mental Health Center. Trained personnel there can also provide buprenorphine, but it is usually understood as a substitute treatment for a short-period of time and the medication is not used for long-term maintenance. While the reasons for this preference in the use medications are not clear, the expert suggests that the use of buprenorphine is not widespread due to local policies, since in China, people who use drugs are defined as both patients and criminal offenders. In addition, early observations, cue that the number of MAT patients is decreasing in China, hence the government does not plan to extend and develop the MAT clinics or diversity in provided medications any further. Other studies from China have also shown that patients reported side-effects and poorer physical health under the treatment with buprenorphine and were more prone to frequent relapses (Shen et al., 2019).

4. *What were the reasons for the decrease in the number of patients?*

One reason for a decrease of patients might be that the administration of methadone was not calculated effectively, because "a *large body of research has demonstrated that a higher methadone dosage is more effective to promote treatment compliance and reduce heroin use [while] under-dosing is one of the predictors for treatment dropout*" (Lee and Newman, 2017). It is also mentioned by Chinese experts, that providers with negative attitudes toward people who use drugs, confusion of treatment objectives and misunderstanding of the comprehensive treatment strategy (including psychological counselling and support) were more likely to be associated with bad treatment consequences. Negative attitudes may play a role by affecting the interaction between the providers and clients (Chen and Zhao, 2019) thereby affecting the trust and subsequently, the retention in the program.

Both in Kazakhstan and Kyrgyzstan, the reasons for termination of the treatment and potential reduction of patients enrolling in MAT are similar. These include low motivation of injecting drug users themselves, environmental factors that lead to unpreparedness to stay in therapy for a long time and abstain from concurrent use of illegal drugs. Experts also report that the majority of MAT clients use the program as an "alternate airfield" meaning if the drugs of choice are not available, many prefer to enroll into the program as an alternative way of drug use. Other reasons for discontinued treatment include transition of clients to other psychoactive substances (NPS), lack of trust and myths about methadone being a poisonous drug that are spread among people who inject drugs and the general population, which negatively affect the motivation to seek treatment with methadone. This lack of motivation is also often accompanied with punitive intervention practices of law enforcement bodies (often detaining patients on the site for no reason).

In addition, mandatory registration at drug treatment centers, with consequent serious restrictions in job market, obtaining a driver's license, the risk of losing custody of children, and the threat of confidentiality also contribute to avoiding MAT altogether. There is also evidence of lack of psychosocial support according to individual needs and unknown state of affairs regarding financing and unresolved tasks of transferring the data to the department of the Ministry of Health. Finally, stigma and discrimination and lack of engagement from the side of organizations working with people who inject drugs, to motivate potential patients to enroll in MAT, are often due to insufficient knowledge and understanding of the real benefits of MAT programs.

5. What impact did law enforcement, medical considerations, general political climate and other, external factors have with regard to the development of MAT programs?

Despite the existing challenges, *China* has made a leap forward in scaling-up the MAT by incorporating patient-centered clinical technologies such as the use of smartphones for easy recovery access (see Schulte et al., 2017), although access to smartphones and surveillance by law enforcement remain as main barriers. Against this background, we argue that China could substantially benefit from adapting the long-term experiences with methadone-maintenance treatment in Hong Kong on a national scale (see Lee & Newman, 2017).

The MAT program in *Kazakhstan* has been in pilot mode since 2008 and is funded by the Global Fund. This year, the program has been renewed until 2023 with the agreement signed between the Ministry of Health of Kazakhstan and the Global Fund signed a grant agreement (azattyq.org, 2021). However, the anti-MAT propaganda in Kazakhstan receives the state's support along several central arguments of the opponents. There is a strong opinion that harm reduction programs, including MAT, is imposed by the West as it also mostly funded by Western money coming through non-governmental organizations (Hieromonk et al., 2007). Opponents of MAT believe that a new type of drug business is created in the country under the cover of such treatment programs (mk-kz.kz, 2019) and that research and clinical trials of methadone in Kazakhstan were conducted in violation of legal requirements to favor OST (mk-kz.kz, 2019; Hieromonk et al., 2007). Experts report that the program has yet to achieve its goal of full re-socialization of people who use drugs (mk-kz.kz, 2019). A review of grey literature suggests that there is also a concern that the methadone program may lead to mass unrest (akzhol.kz, 2017), as these fears were reignited following a failure of methadone supply in Temirtau with patients showing "withdrawal" symptoms manifested in aggression, depression, pain, and disruption of family relationships (zakon.kz, n.d.). Other opponents lead by the example from Russia and Uzbekistan who refused the MAT program. The familiar fear of promotional effect of the use of methadone leading to heavier forms of drug with more devastating consequences remains as popular. Despite these oppositions in society at large and in government cabinets, the Ministry of Health adopted a new order in 2019 approving the "Roadmap for the Implementation of a Supportive Substitution Therapy Program for Opioid Dependents in the Republic of Kazakhstan for 2019–2020".

6. Which role did NGOs play with respect to psycho-social support of MAT patients?

Our review of literature shows that in *Kazakhstan*, more than 1,500 NGOs that receive government funding are registered on the official websites of the "Center for the Support of Civic Initiatives" and public procurement of Kazakhstan. More than 200 NGOs are registered on the official website of the "Center for the Support of Civic Initiatives" (cisc.kz, 2021). The mission of the center is to assist NGOs in the implementation of social projects of the state.

The "Center for Support of Civic Initiatives" for 2017–2021 covers a total of 308 projects, of which 84 (27.3 %) are aimed at promoting civil society organizations, 55 (17.8 %) are engaged in youth policy and children's initiatives, 54 (17.5 %) in the protection of rights and legal interests of citizens and organizations, 16 (5.2 %) focus on achieving goals in education, science, information, physical culture and sports, and 8 (2.5 %) are in the field of health and promotion of healthy lifestyles (cisc.kz, 2021).

These initiatives are complemented with the analysis of the official website of public procurement of Kazakhstan in 2021 shows 1,826 procurement announcements on the state social order (goszakup.gov.kz, 2021). According to the law on the "State Social Order, Grants and Awards for NGOs in the Republic of Kazakhstan" of 12 April 2005, the state social order is a form of social programs, social projects, functions of central and (or) local executive bodies transferred for implementation in a competitive environment, aimed at solving problems in the social sphere, performed by NGOs from budgetary funds.

The analysis of the interviewed experts showed that the state social procurement announcements counts only to 1.1 % out of 1,826 announcements which were aimed at preventing HIV infection and drug addiction. Only one announcement (0,05 %) out of these refers to providing support for people who use drugs. Review of the grey literature showed that for social support of this cohort and on the implementation of measures on prevention among people who inject drugs for 2021, there are no projects with budget funding, and with only three projects are being implemented (in Almaty) supported by foreign donor organization (infonpo.gov.kz).

This overview provides initial insight into possible barriers and facilitators affecting the overall MAT environment in Kazakhstan.

In the *Kyrgyzstan*, nongovernmental organizations are successfully working to promote the social reintegration of MAT patients. At different times of the existence of the substitution therapy program, the non-governmental sector was actively involved in providing services and assistance to clients in different areas of life (e.g. RANAR PF "Healthy Generation" PF "Flagman Project" PF "Parents Against Drugs" Harm Reduction Network Association, "Sotsium", "Alternative in Narcology", etc. The NGO "Alternative in Narcology", organized by MAT patients themselves, which conducts self-help groups for patients and provides a range of social and psychological assistance to PTM patients and their relatives, can be especially noteworthy.

7. Which role play Social Work with respect to psycho-social support of MAT patients?

In PR China there was no social work in the development of the "socialist society"; it was not considered necessary because the neighbourhood committees in the residential districts of the factories largely took care of all social problems of the population – including relationship and family problems, educational and school questions – right up to the very clear "social control" against "deviant" and so-called "anti-social" behaviour as a metaphor for any individualistic positioning towards the collective idea, which has long been deeply anchored in Asian societies.

In addition, there is no history of charities and non-governmental organizations in China that attempt to regulate social conflicts in a non-state manner.

Government action is defined positivistically as a legitimate claim (of the state or society) to resolve social and personal conflicts. Social work is subordinate to it by definition: Angelina Yuen-Tsang – one of the leading theorists of social work in China defines this ascription:

> *"A characteristic feature of social work education in China is a close relationship with the Central Government which has played, and is still playing, a pivotal role in the planning and development of social policies and social services in China. The voluntary sector is only just emerging and its contribution to social welfare development has been relatively insignificant in the past. "* (Yuen-Tsin, 2008))

This relationship is also characterized by the fact that social workers are largely state employees who work within government-compliant bureaucracy. *"Social workers educators are actively involved in government projects as honorary advisors, consultants and trainers."* (Yuen-Tsin, 2008)

The basic idea behind this is the objective of leaving the *academic ivory tower* and positively interfering in social developments: the programme's curriculum of the China Association of Social Work provides an „*education model which emphasizes theory-practice integration, critical reflection, action learning, culturally sensitive practice and commitment to social change and development."* (Yuen-Tsin, 2008)

The institutionalization of social work as a university faculty/discipline in China was based *"as a pragmatic solution to social problems and as a way to stabilize society following the introduction of the open door economic policy and the market economy"*. (Yuen-Tsin, 2008) in the late 1980ies (with the aim to establish a "harmonious society" [even according to traditional Chinese history of confuzianism])., because in the starting phase social work educators were transferred from disciplines such as history, anthropology, sociology and philosophy, so social work had been reintroduced into universities by academics with neither the professional expertise nor the practical experience to develop this newly introduced professional discipline.

Whereas China has started more than 20 years ago with this institutionalization of social work education, the post-soviet Central Asian countries are just in the starting phase of this process.

But "professional colonization" – using Western role models (from United States, UK, Northern European countries) or "Westernized neighbours" (such as Hong Kong or Taiwan) had been part of the "globalization process" (supported by ais programs from US and UK or Australia), but China's social work educators had been struggling to *develop "local, culturally appropriate programmes, while constantly torn between the conflicting tensions of professionalization and bureaucratization"*. (Yuen-Tsin, 2008)

Research as Social Practice

> *"In many of their practicum projects, students adopted integrated action research approach, using participatory research methods, applying ethnographic methods to collect oral histories and to generate local knowledge and relevant practice models in partnership with local communities"*. (Yuen-Tsin, 2008)

As social work (and research on social work) with drug users/dependents is still in the embryonic state – both in China and in Central Asia – our SOLID project can be used to implement such (research) experiences in this field (of research and action). (Yuen-Tsin, 2008)

This overview is based on the experiences both of the EU CADAP programme (CADAP, 2020) as well on the DAAD exceed programme "Social work and strengthening NGOs in development cooperation to treat drug addiction" a jointly developed research program on the influence of social work on the prevention and treatment of drug addiction with the main focus on role of NGOs. (www.solid-exceed.org)

Conclusion

Despite the WHO-recommended low-threshold approach to MAT in all countries, the enrolment and eligibility criteria in both Central Asia and China remain complicated (Chen & Zhao, 2019; Latypov et al., 2010; Yan et al., 2013). The most recent review of the MAT in Central Asia shows that these barriers identified a decade ago continue to persist to this day (Author, 2020). Under 5 % of the injecting drug user cohort have been covered by the intermittent MAT in all Central Asian countries, albeit the treatment has been terminated in Uzbekistan completely since 2009 (Author, 2021). In China, the situation varies generally from province to province, although there are general barriers such as lack of psychological counselling and misconceptions about MAT among the staff and the patients (Wang et al., 2014).

As before, the political will in both regions and adequate funding remain the central prerequisites for achieving success in harm reduction measures (UNODC, 2020). The Global Fund is the main donor (60 %) of harm reduction measures in the regions with NGOs receiving the most amount of financial support and community organizations, although to a lesser degree (Serebryakova et al., 2021). Our data and analyses showed that in both China and Central Asia, there are similar barriers in accessing effective MAT. At its core, these barriers often come from strict state and institutional regulations preventing easy access, which is partially explained by ongoing distrust in the effectiveness of harm reduction policies. This article, hence, showed that struggling to integrate crucial harm reduction measures and medication-assisted treatment of drug use, local governments face challenges of preserving the prohibitionist laws and therefore, enforcing resultant zero-tolerance drug policies, all the while trying to adapt to changing global drug control landscape which increasingly promotes harm reduction as a basic human right. While Western donors operate on the basis of international consensus on human-rights-based harm reduction approaches, of which MAT is one part, they often fall short in adjusting the programs in culturally-appropriate ways and with consideration of local political and social discourse. Hence, the above discussed political barriers preventing a better and successful implementation of basic harm reduction programs are not only challenging for local governments, but are also responsibilities for better functioning international cooperation and global sustainability goals.

References

Абишев, А. Т. (2020). Анализ состояния дерматовенерологической службы Республики Казахстан итогам 2020 года. *Вопросы дерматологии и Венерологии* (1–2), 29–36.

azattyq.org. (15 07 2021 г.). Получено из Метадон: зло или благо? Что будет с заместительной терапией для наркозависимых: https://rus.azattyq.org/a/kazakh stan-methadone-drug-addiction-treatment-project/31356654.html

akzhol.kz. (24 05 2017 г.). Почему наркотик «Метадон», запрещенный Конвенцией ООН к применению в медицинских целях, официально используется у нас в качестве препарата заместительной терапии? Получено из Официальный сайт Демократической партии «Ак жол»: https://akzhol.kz/ru/migrated_4694/

Azbel, L., Rozanova, J., Michels, I., Altice, F. L., & Stöver, H. (2017). A qualitative assessment of an abstinence-oriented therapeutic community for prisoners with substance use disorders in Kyrgyzstan. Harm Reduction Journal, 14(1), 1- 9. https://doi.org/10.1186/s12954-017-0168-8

Bakirova Zh (2021): paper on from 13th September 2021: Бакирова Жылдыз: Информация для включения в статью Барьеры и посредники на пути медикаментозного лечения потребителей опиоидов в Центральной Азии и Китае» (Bakirova Jyldyz: Information for inclusion in the article Barriers and intermediaries to drug treatment of opioid users in Central Asia and China")

Central Asia Drug Action Programme (CADAP), phase 6; Final Report; DCI-ASIE/2015/356–893; Bishkek/Brussels; March 2020

Central Asia Human Development Report: Bringing Down Barriers (http://europe andcis.undp.org/governance/hrj/show/300BDC00-F203-1EE9-BE944F24EDFC0 9CE)

cisc.kz. (21 Июнь 2021 г.). ПРОЕКТЫ НАО Центр поддержки гражданских инициатив. Получено из НАО Центр поддержки гражданских инициатив: https://cisc.kz/ru/projects/?_projects_theme=6c05744a6ba3f84c21334f66f2e1 6521

Chen T, Zhao M. (2019): Meeting the challenges of opioid dependence in China: Experience of opioid agonist treatment. In Current Opinion in Psychiatry (Vol. 32, Issue 4, pp. 282–287). Lippincott Williams and Wilkins. https://doi.org/10.10 97/YCO.0000000000000509

Cherchenko N (2021): paper on from 13th September 2021: Information for inclusion in the article Barriers and intermediaries to drug treatment of opioid users in Central Asia and China "

Dong, R., Wang, H., Li, D., Lang, L., Gray, F., Liu, Y., Laffont, C. M., Young, M., Jiang, J., Liu, Z., & Learned, S. M. (2019). Pharmacokinetics of Sublingual Buprenorphine Tablets Following Single and Multiple Doses in Chinese Participants With and Without Opioid Use Disorder. *Drugs in R and D, 19*(3), 255–265. https://doi.org/10.1007/s40268-019-0277-9

European Monitoring Centre for Drugs and Drug Addiction (EMCDDA). (2021). *Balancing access to opioid substitution treatment with preventing the diversion of opioid substitution medications in Europe: challenges and implications* (Issue February). https://www.emcdda.europa.eu/publications/technical-reports/opioid-substitution-treatment-ost-in-europe-availability-and-diversion_en

EU Drugs Strategy (2013–20) (2012/C 402/01) Official Journal of the European Union, 29.12.2012; EU Drugs Strategy 2021–2025, Council of the European Union, CORDROGUE 80 SAN 483 COSI 255 RELEX 1026 UD 399, Brussels, 18 December 2020; EU-Central Asia Action Plan on Drugs (2014–2020), Council of the European Union, 18020/13 CORDROGUE 139 COEST 417, Brussels, 1 October 2013

International standards for the treatment of drug use disorders: revised edition incorporating results of field-testing; Geneva: World Health Organization and United Nations Office on Drugs and Crime; 2020. License: CC BY-NC-SA 3.0 IGO; ISBN 978–92–4–000219–7 (electronic version) ISBN 978–92–4–000220–3 (print version)

informburo.kz. (11 06 2017 г.). Получено 2021, из Пункт бесплатной выдачи метадона откроют в наркодиспансере Атырау: https://informburo.kz/novosti/p unkt-besplatnoy-vydachi-metadona-otkroyut-v-narkodispansere-atyrau.html

Grella, C. E., Ostile, E., Scott, C. K., Dennis, M., & Carnavale, J. (2020). A Scoping Review of Barriers and Facilitators to Implementation of Medications for Treatment of Opioid Use Disorder within the Criminal Justice System. In *International Journal of Drug Policy* (Vol. 81, p. 102768). Elsevier B.V. https://doi.org/1 0.1016/j.drugpo.2020.102768

Harm Reduction International. (2014). *The Global State of Harm Reduction 2014* (K. A. Stone (ed.)). Harm Reduction International.

Hedrich, D., Pirona, A., & Wiessing, L. (2008). From margin to mainstream: The evolution of harm reduction responses to problem drug use in Europe. *Drugs: Education, Prevention and Policy, 15*(6), 503–517. https://doi.org/10.1080/0968763 0802227673

Hieromon, A.V., Shvetsova, Y.B., & Kaklyugin, N.V. (2007). ОСТОРОЖНО – МЕТАДОН!!! Получено. из http://www.blaivus.org/UserFiles/blaivi_karta/14.3. %20Pakaitinis%20gydymas%20metadonu/539atsargiai4.pdf

Jolley E, Rhodes T, Platt L, et al. HIV among people who inject drugs in Central and Eastern Europe and Central Asia: a systematic review with implications for policy. BMJ Open 2012;2: e001465. doi:10.1136/ bmjopen-2012–001465

LaMonaca, K., Dumchev, K., Dvoriak, S., Azbel, L., Morozova, O., & Altice, F. L. (2019). HIV, Drug Injection, and Harm Reduction Trends in Eastern Europe and Central Asia: Implications for International and Domestic Policy. In *Current Psychiatry Reports* (Vol. 21, Issue 7). Current Medicine Group LLC 1. https:// doi.org/10.1007/s11920-019-1038-8

Latypov, A., et al. Illicit drugs in Central Asia: What we know, what we don't know, and what we need to know. International Journal of Drug Policy.2014 http://dx.doi.org/10.1016/j.drugpo.2014.09.015http://dx.doi.org/10.1016/j.drugp o.2014.09.015

Latypov, A. (2010). Opioid substitution therapy in Tajikistan: Another perpetual pilot? *International Journal of Drug Policy*, 21(5), 407–410. https://doi.org/10.1016 /j.drugpo.2010.01.013

Latypov, A., Otiashvili, D., Aizberg, O., & Boltaev, A. (2010). *Opioid Substitution Therapy in Central Asia: Towards diverse and effective treatment options for drug dependence*

Lee, S. & Newman, R. (2017): Methadone maintenance — lessons from two systems in China. Harm Reduction Journal, 14(66), 1–5. https://doi.org/10.1186/s1 2954-017-0193-7

Lucas, G. M., Beauchamp, G., Aramrattana, A., Shao, Y., Liu, W., Fu, L., Jackson, J. B., Celentano, D. D., Richardson, P., & Metzger, D. (2012). Short-term safety of buprenorphine/naloxone in HIV-seronegative opioid-dependent Chinese and Thai drug injectors enrolled in HIV Prevention Trials Network 058. *International al Journal of Drug Policy*, 23(2), 162–165. https://doi.org/10.1016/j.drugpo.2011.0 6.005

Lu L, Wang X. Drug Addiction in China. Ann N Y Acad Sci. 2008; 1141:304–317

Meise M, Wang X, Sauter ML, Bao Y-p, Shi J, Liu Z-m, Lu L. Harm reduction for injecting opiate users: an update and implications in China. Acta Pharmacologica Sinica. 2009; 30:513–521

Marienfelda M, Liub P, Wang X, Schottenfelda R, Zhoub W, Chawarskia M (2015); Evaluation of an Implementation of Methadone Maintenance Treatment in China; Drug Alcohol Depend. December 1; 157: 60–67. doi:10.1016/j.drugalcdep.2015.10.001.

MacArthur, G. J., Minozzi, S., Martin, N., Vickerman, P., Deren, S., Bruneau, J., Degenhardt, L., & Hickman, M. (2012). Opiate substitution treatment and HIV transmission in people who inject drugs: Systematic review and meta-analysis. In *BMJ (Online)* (Vol. 345, Issue 7879). British Medical Journal Publishing Group. https://doi.org/10.1136/bmj.e5945

Mattick, R. P., Breen, C., Kimber, J., & Davoli, M. (2009). Methadone maintenance therapy versus no opioid replacement therapy for opioid dependence. In *Cochrane Database of Systematic Reviews* (Vol. 2009, Issue 3). John Wiley and Sons Ltd. https://doi.org/10.1002/14651858.CD002209.pub2

Michels II, Fang Y, Zhao Zh, Dong, Zhao L, Lu L (2007): Comparison of drug abuse in Germany and China; Acta Pharmacol Sin, Oct; 28 (10): 1505–151

Michels II, Zhao M, Lu L (2007): Drug abuse and its treatment in China; SUCHT,53 (4), 228–237; DOI 10.1463/2007.04.04

Michels II, Keizer B, Trautmann F, Stöver H, Robelló E (2017): Improvement of Treatment of Drug use Disorders in Central Asia the contribution of the EU Central Asia Drug Action Programme (CADAP). J Addict Med Ther 5(1): 1025

Michels II, Stöver H, Aizberg O, Boltaev, A (2021): Opioid Agonist Treatment for Opioid Use Disorder patients in Central Asia; Heroin Addiction and Related Clinical Problems, March 2021

National Health and Family Planning Commission of the People's Republic of China. May 2015. Retrieved 18 February 2020

National Institute on Drug Abuse (NIDA). (2021). *Words Matter: Terms to Use and Avoid When Talking About Addiction*. NIDAMED. https://www.drugabuse.gov/ni damed-medical-health-professionals/health-professions-education/words-matter-t erms-to-use-avoid-when-talking-about-addiction

Parsons, D., Burrows, D., & Bolotbaeva, A. (2014). Advocating for opioid substitution therapy in Central Asia: Much still to be done. *International Journal of Drug Policy*, 25(6), 1174–1177. https://doi.org/10.1016/j.drugpo.2014.01.004

Serebryakova, L., Cook, C., & Davies, C. (2021). *Failure to fund: The continued crisis for harm reduction funding in low-and middle-income countries* (Issue May).

Subata E, Moeller L, Karymbaeva S (2016): Evaluation of opioid substitution therapy in Kyrgyzstan; WHO Regional Office, Copenhagen

Sun H-M, , Li X-Y, Chow EP, Xian Y, Lu, Y-H, Tian T, Zhuan X, Zhang L, (2015): Methadone maintenance treatment reduces criminal activity and improves social well.being of drug users in China: a systematic review and meta-analysis. BMJ Open 2015; 5; e005997. Doi:10.1136/bmopen-2014-005997

Shen J, Yu DB (2005): Governmental policies on HIV infection in China. Cell Res. 2005; 15:903–907

Shen, W., Wang, Q., Zhang, J., Ping, W., Zhang, J., Ye, W., Hu, Q., Cerci, D., & Zhou, W. (2019). A Retrospective Survey of Buprenorphine Substitute Treatment With Minimal Dosage in Heroin Use Disorder. *Frontiers in Psychiatry*, 10(December), 1–8. https://doi.org/10.3389/fpsyt.2019.00888

Schulte, M., Liang, D., Wu, F., Lan, Y.-C., Tsay, W., Du, J., Zhao, M., Li, X., & Hser, Y. (2017). A smartphone application supporting recovery from heroin addiction: Perspectives of patients and providers in China, Taiwan, and the USA. *Physiology & Behavior*, 176(3), 139–148. https://doi.org/10.1007/s11481-016 -9653-1.A

Stöver, H. (2010). Barriers to opioid substitution treatment access, entry and retention: A survey of opioid users, patients in treatment, and treating and non-treating physicians. *European Addiction Research*, 17(1), 44–54. https://doi.org/10.1159 /000320576

Sullivan, S. G., Wu, Z., Cao, X., Liu, E., & Detels, R. (2014). Continued drug use during methadone treatment in China: A retrospective analysis of 19,026 service users. *J Subst Abuse Treat*, *47*(1), 86–92. https://doi.org/10.1016/j.jsat.2013.12.004. Continued

Sultan, A. (2018). *Overlooked youth: How does national drug discourse influence recovery in Azerbaijan?* Baku Research Institute. https://bakuresearchinstitute.org/overlooked-youth-how-does-national-drug-discourse-influence-recovery-in-azerbaijan/

Sullivan S, Wu Z. Rapid scale up of harm reduction in China. Int J Drug Policy. 2007; 18:118–128.

The Regional Report on the Drug Situation in Central Asia was prepared within the framework of the Central Asia Drug Action Programme; Prague 2019 (ISBN 978–80–907417–8–2)

United Nations Office on Drugs and Crime. (2020). *World Drug Report*. www.unodc.org/wdr2020

UNGASS 2016 outcome document "Our joint commitment to effectively addressing and countering the world drug problem": "We recognize that the world drug problem remains a common and shared responsibility that should be addressed in a multilateral setting through effective and increased international cooperation and demands an integrated, multidisciplinary, mutually reinforcing, balanced, scientific evidence-based and comprehensive approach". United Nations, Vienna, June 2016, p 2

Wang, L., Wei, X., Wang, X., Li, J., Li, H., & Jia, W. (2014). Long-term effects of methadone maintenance treatment with different psychosocial intervention models. *PLoS ONE*, *9*(2), 1–8. https://doi.org/10.1371/journal.pone.0087931

World Health Organization. (2014). How to improve Opioid Substitution Therapy implementation: Experiences from EU countries, part of a join EAHC-WHO project involving Bulgaria, Estonia, Germany, Latvia, Lithuania, Poland, Portugal and Romania (Issue January). http://www.euro.who.int/__data/assets/pdf_file/0015/241341/How-to-improve-Opioid-Substitution-Therapy-implementation.pdf?ua=1:

WHO: Guidelines for the psychosocially assisted pharmacological treatment of opioid dependence; Geneva 2009 ISBN 978 92 4 154754 3

Yan, L., Liu, E., McGoogan, J. M., Duan, S., Wu, L. T., Comulada, S., & Wu, Z. (2013). Referring heroin users from compulsory detoxification centers to community methadone maintenance treatment: A comparison of three models. *BMC Public Health*, *13*(1), 1–8. https://doi.org/10.1186/1471-2458-13-747

Yuen-Tsin A, KU B (2008): A journey of a Thousand Miles begins with One Step: the development of culturally relevant Social Work Education and fieldwork practice in China; In: Mel Gray et.al (ed).: Indigenous Social Work around the world. Towards culturally relevant education and practice; New York 2016 (first edition 2008)

Yin W, Hao Y, Sun X, Gong X, Li F, Li J, Rou K, Sullivan SG, Wang C, Cao X, Luo W, Wu Z. (2019): Scaling up the national methadone maintenance treatment program in China: achievements and challenges. Int J Epidemiol. 2010; 39:ii29–ii37

zakon.kz. (n.d.). Получено из Граждане Казахстана выступают против продвижения наркотика «метадон», как средства для «лечения» наркозависимых. Accessed August 29, 2021 via https://online.zakon.kz/Document/?doc_id=30955906#pos=19;-12

Zabransky, T., Mravcik, V., Talu, A., & Jasaitis, E. (2014). Post-Soviet Central Asia: A summary of the drug situation. *International Journal of Drug Policy*, 25(6), 1186–1194. https://doi.org/10.1016/j.drugpo.2014.05.004

Zhang G, Yang Y, Ye R, Zhang D, Shan D, Hu Y, Dai B, Liu Zh (2018): Effect of community-based extension clinics of methadone maintenance therapy for opiate-dependent clients. Medicine (2018) 97:47 (e13323) http://dx.doi.org/10.1097/MD.0000000000013323

Zhang L, Zou X, Xu Y, Medland N, Deng L, Liu Y, Su S, Ling L (2019): The decade-long Chinese Methadone Maintenance Therapy yields large population and economic benefits for drug users in reducing harm, HIV and HCV disease burden, Fron tiers in Public Health 7:327. Doi: 10.3389/fpubh.2019.00327

Zhang, J. Y., Li, Z. Bin, Zhang, L., Wang, J., Huang, L. P., Zhan, G. L., Li, Z., Du, J., & Zhao, M. (2019). DOES IT WORK? -a randomized controlled trial to test the efficacy of HCV and HIV-related education on drug users in MMT, China. *BMC Infectious Diseases*, 19(1), 774. https://doi.org/10.1186/s12879-019-4421-5

Zhao M (2029): Drug Addiction treatment and rehabilitation in China; presentation at Solid-Exceed October School 2020 on 28 October 2020 at Solid-Exceed – Courses in a Track (solid-exceed.org)

Zhong N, Yuan Y, Chen H, Jiang H, Du J, Sun, H, Hao W, Zhao M (2015): Effects of a Randomized Comprehensive Psychosocial Intervention Based on Cognitive Behavioral Therapy Theory and Motivational Interviewing Techniques for Community Rehabilitation of Patients With Opioid Use Disorders in Shanghai, China; J Addict Med 2015;9: 322–330 ISSN: 1932–0620/15/0904–0322 DOI: 10.1097/ADM.0000000000000139

PART III

Developments in the Role of Social Work in the treatment of drug addicted people in Central Asia and China

Social work and strengthening of NGOs in development cooperation to treat drug addiction[*]

*Ingo Ilja Michels[**,1], Heino Stöver[2], Nurgul Musaeva[3], Dinara Yessimova[4], Jiang Du[5], Azizbek Boltaev[6], Subkhon Ashuro, and Umeda Munavvarova[7,8]*

Abstract

Social work is one of the youngest scientific disciplines, it has developed itself as a discipline to address individuals, families and communities in social crisis (poverty, low level of education, un- employment, diseases, social isolation). In the last decade also problems with alcohol and drug dependencies increasingly became the subject of social work support(systems). Due to coming globalisation, where living space has become wider than the community itself, social work was forced to operate within wider horizons and to go beyond communities boundaries. Social work nowadays has been becoming a more global scientific discipline seeking answers to global questions. Social work is therefore linked to all seventeen global

[*] First Published in International Journal of Addiction Research and Therapy, IJART, 2021; 4:25.

[**] [1]Frankfurt University of Applied Sciences, Institute for Drug Research (Frankfurt, Germany), International Scientific Coordinator for the SOLID project. [2]Frankfurt University of Applied Sciences, Institute for Drug Research (Frankfurt, Germany), Professor for Social Work and Health, Project Leader of the SOLID project. [3]Bishkek State University, Department of Social Work and Practical Psychology (Bishkek, Kyrgyzstan), Scientific Coordinator for the SOLID project. [4]Eurasian National University Gumilyov, Department of Sociology (Astana / Nur-Sultan, Kazakhstan), Scientific Coordinator for the SOLID project. [5]Shanghai Mental Health Centre, Shanghai Jiaotong University School of Medicine (Shanghai, PR China), Scientific Coordinator for the SOLID project. [6]Bukhara State Medical Institute (Bukhara, Uzbekistan), Scientific Coordinator for the SOLID project. [7/8] Caritas Tajikistan, Doctor of Economics (former Vice Minister of Labour and Social Protection), Dushanbe & Caritas Tajikistan, (PhD for Social Work, former Associate Professor at Tajik National Medical University), (Dushanbe, Tajikistan).

goals of sustainable development (SDGs). As the prevention and treatment of drug addiction in Germany and Central Asia has reached a common urgency, a training and research project in the field of social work in addiction support was developed in Germany, Central Asian countries (Kazakhstan, Kyrgyzstan, Uzbekistan, Tajikistan) and China. The development of social work in these countries increasingly led to the development of common principles in the technology and ethics of social work, comparing standards and working out the socio-cultural peculiarities in the definition and practice of social work. These developments are examined and presented and their common solution ideas discussed in the con- text of achieving the UN Sustainable Development Goals.

Keywords: Social work; treat drug addiction

1. Introduction

The Central Asian (CA) countries Kazakhstan, the Kyrgyz Republic, Tajikistan, Turkmenistan, and Uzbekistan – include more than 60 million ethnically, culturally, and religiously diverse people distributed over a geographical area twice the size of continental Europe, getting independent when the Soviet Union dissolved in 1991.[1] Since independence, they have faced the huge challenges such as inappropriate and unaffordable health systems.[2] Many different groups have a role to play: national politicians and local governments, the health professions, the scientific community, the private sector and civil society organizations, as well as the global health community. Today, Central Asia (CA) has become a key region for

---

1 Central Asia Human Development Report: Bringing Down Barriers (http://europ eandcis.undp.org/governance/hrj/show/300BDC00-F203-1EE9-BE944F24EDFC0 9CE).

2 "End of the Soviet rule came with the collapse of the cen-tralised economy and political transformations in all of the Central Asian states. Regime transition from centralised to market economy and democratisation of newly formed post-Soviet societies was greatly expected. Early post-So-viet times saw declining living standards, weakening pub-lic health infrastructure, and decline in life expectancy among others in most of the Central Asian region (...) The public health situation has been deteriorating in all of the Central Asian Republics and the system of health care built by Soviets has completely collapsed by now. Epi-demic picture of the region worsened through increased migration, poverty, absence of quality health services and mismanagement in all levels of decision making systems." [Turaeva M.: (2019): "HIV/AIDS and Drug Abuse in post- Soviet Central Asia: Soviet style of biopolitics and health regimes." PhD diss., University of Bielefeld]

the international activities tackling illegal drugs and related problems – specifically the problems with illicit opioids, and increasingly, also cannabinoids. Drugs and drug related problems, such as crimes, dependency or infectious diseases (such as HIV/AIDS, hepatitis, and TB) are key challenges for the international community and each state.[3] The European Union has supported the CA countries' for several years to support a balanced drug policy in line with the EU Drug Strategy 2013–2020, EU Drug Strategy 2021–2030 and the EU Central Asia Drug Action Plan 2014–2020[4]. According to the annual reports of the drug situation in 2012 and 2013 and recently 2018[5] there are first signs of a reduction of drug dependency and infectious diseases (at least of the officially registered persons with drug dependence or infectious diseases such as HIV/AIDS and Hepatitis C). It is difficult to analyse the reasons for this trend, but it can be stabilized by a common initiative of CA countries to tackle these drug related problems on a regional level. All countries in Central Asia are supporting the common view of the UN bodies (UN Drug Convention 1961, Art. 38; and Political Declaration 2009) to implement all practicable measures for *"prevention, early identification; treatment, education, after-care and rehabilitation and social reintegration"* of drug dependent people and the UNGASS outcome document from 2016.[6] The same is true for the PR Chi-

---

3 Michels II, Keizer B, Trautmann F, Stöver H, Robelló E (2017) Improvement of Treatment of Drug use Disorders in Central Asia the contribution of the EU Central Asia Drug Action Programme (CADAP). J Addict Med Ther 5(1): 1025.

4 EU Drugs Strategy (2013–20) (2012/C 402/01) Official Journal of the European Union, 29.12.2012; EU Drugs Strategy 2021–2025, Council of the European Union, CORDROGUE 80 SAN 483 COSI 255 RELEX 1026 UD 399, Brussels, 18 December 2020; EU-Central Asia Action Plan on Drugs (2014–2020), Council of the European Union, 18020/13 CORDROGUE 139 COEST 417, Brussels, 1 October 2013.

5 The Regional Report on the Drug Situation in Central Asia was prepared within the framework of the Central Asia Drug Action Programme; Prague 2019 (ISBN 978–80–907417–8–2) and Zabransky T, Mravcik V, Talu A, Jasaitis E. Post-Soviet Central Asia: a summary of the drug situation. Int J Drug Policy. 2014; 25: 1186–1194; see also: Jolley E, Rhodes T, Platt L, et al. HIV among people who inject drugs in Central and Eastern Europe and Central Asia: a systematic review with implications for policy. BMJ Open 2012;2: e001465. doi:10.1136/ bmjopen-2012–001465 or Latypov, A., et al. Illicit drugs in Central Asia: What we know, what we don't know, and what we need to know. International Journal of Drug Policy. 2014 http://dx.doi.org/10.1016/j.drugpo.2014.09.015http://dx.doi.org/10.1016/j.dru gpo.2014.09.015.

6 According to the UNGASS 2016 outcome document "Our joint commitment to effectively addressing and countering the world drug problem": *"We recognize that the world drug problem remains a common and shared responsibility that should be ad-*

na. The number of registered drug users increased from 70,000 in 1990 to more than 2,8 mio.by the end of 2018. One major drug-related problem has been the spread of HIV. Figures from the Chinese Center for Disease Control and Prevention, World Health Organization, and UNAIDS estimate that there were 1.25 million people living with HIV/AIDS in China at the end of 2018, with 135,000 new infections from 2017[7]. The reported incidence of HIV/AIDS in China is relatively low. About 50 % of them are injecting drug users, but Sexual transmission gradually began to overtake the originally predominant routes of transmission. Since 2003, China has implemented harm-reduction measures such as needle-and-syringe programmes and methadone maintenance treatment for controlling the spread of HIV/AIDS. Although compulsory treatment options are still mostly used, voluntary treatment facilities are growing rapidly, and psychotherapeutic treatment options are being implemented.[8] Also in China we recognize

> „still a large number of drug users (…) although the growth rate has slowed down. The major abused drugs are methamphetamine, heroin and ketamine. The abuse of synthetic drugs such as methamphetamine continues to increase, with 80 % of newly discovered users abusing synthetic drugs. Among traditional drugs, heroin abuse increase is slowing".[9]

In both, Central Asian countries as well as in the PR China modern methods of treatment of drug use disorders, according to the UNODC/WHO International Standards of treatment of drug use disorders[10] have been im-

---

dressed in a multilateral setting through effective and increased international cooperation and demands an integrated, multidisciplinary, mutually reinforcing, balanced, scientific evidence-based and comprehensive approach". United Nations, Vienna, June 2016, p.2.

7 National Health and Family Planning Commission of the People's Republic of China. May 2015. Retrieved 18 February 2020.

8 Michels I.I., Zhao M., Lu L. (2007): Drug abuse and its treatment in China; Such, 53 (4), 228–237; DOI 10.1463/2007.04.04.

9 Zhao Min, Drug Addiction treatment and rehabilitation in China; presentation at Solid-Exceed October School 2020 on 28 October 2020 at Solid-Exceed – Courses in a Track (solid-exceed.org).

10 International standards for the treatment of drug use disorders: revised edition incorporating results of field-testing; Geneva: World Health Organization and United Nations Office on Drugs and Crime; 2020. License: CC BY-NC-SA 3.0 IGO; ISBN 978–92–4–000219–7 (electronic version) ISBN 978–92–4–000220–3 (print version).

plemented[11][12], including Opioid Substitution Treatment (OST), although the provision of treatment is limited and not affordable for those in need and psycho-social assistance is still widely not available.[13] Especially social work is missing or still in an infancy phase.

2. What is social work about?

"Social work is a profession built on hope—hope for change, hope for a better life for abused and neglected children, the poor, the sick, the disabled, and the elderly. The sobering reality is that the values of freedom, justice, social responsibility, and human dignity drive a profession that of-ten goes unrecognized and underappreciated, even pitied. Because of this, social workers worldwide face an uphill battle, striving to educate and retain a workforce that grapples with compassion fatigue while barely squeaking out a livable wage." (Tappan 2012)

"Social work is one of the youngest scientific disciplines, from which it was not automatically expected to offer broader thinking about society. Regardless such positioning, social work has developed itself as a discipline according to addressing of individuals and wider environment at the same time. Social work was initially placed to address individuals and families, and accordingly communities. Due to coming globalisation, where living space has become wider than the community itself, social work was forced to operate within wider horizons and to go beyond com-munities

---

11 Michels, Ingo Ilja; Zhao, Min; Lu, Lin, Drug abuse and its treatment in China; SUCHT,53 (4), 228–237, 2007 and Michels, Ingo Ilja; Fang, Yu-xia; Zhao, Zhao, Dong; Zhao, Li-yan; Lu, Lin: Comparison of drug abuse in Germany and China; Acta Pharmacol Sin 2007 Oct; 28 (10): 1505–151.

12 Central Asia Drug Action Programme (CADAP), phase 6; Final Report; DCI-ASIE/2015/356–893; Bishkek/Brussels; March 2020.

13 WHO: Guidelines for the psychosocially assisted pharmacological treatment of opioid dependence; Geneva 2009 ISBN 978 92 4 154754 3; see also: Zhong, Na;.Yuan Ying; Chen, Hanhui; Jiang, Haifeng; Du,Jiang; Sun, Haiming; Hao, Wei and Zhao, Min: Effects of a Randomized Comprehensive Psychosocial Intervention Based on Cognitive Behavioral Therapy Theory and Motivational Interviewing Techniques for Community Rehabilitation of Patients With Opioid Use Disorders in Shanghai, China; J Addict Med 2015;9: 322–330 ISSN: 1932–0620/15/0904–0322 DOI: 10.1097/ADM.0000000000000139; see also: Michels, In-go Ilja Michels; Stöver, Heino; Aizberg Oleg, and Boltaev, Azizbek: Opioid Agonist Treatment for Opioid Use Disorder patients in Central Asia; Heroin Addiction and Related Clinical Problems March 2020.

boundaries. Therefore we can claim that social work nowadays has been becoming more and more global scientific discipline since, just like other more established sciences, seeks answers to global questions. Social work is therefore linked to all seventeen global goals of sustainable development." (Hrovatic, 2020)

"Primitive forms of social work appeared in tribal society in the form of an institution of mutual assistance to each other. In the process of historical development, its structure and content were enriched, forms and directions, goals and functional significance expanded, the theoretical, methodological and legal foundations developed, etc. To date, social work has acquired a broad semantic meaning that does not have an unambiguous interpretation. It is seen as social phenomenon, social institution, area of scientific knowledge, social policy implementation mechanism, professional and volunteer activities, the art of overcoming life's difficulties, educational discipline, etc. There are also various approaches and models, orienting specialists in social work versatile approach to solving social problems. This provision requires systematizing theoretical provisions and creating a unified concept understanding the essence of social work. Social work is a unified system of activity structural elements, public relations, institutions with its internal logic of development and a certain integrity. All structural components of social work: object, subject, goals, types, directions, levels, methods, functions, values, principles, etc. complement each other and ensure well-coordinated work on the achievement of the common goal of alleviating and preventing social tensions and establishing social harmony and ensuring stable social development of society". (Musaeva, 2012b)

3. Baseline of Social Work development in Germany

The subject of social work seems to be vague in its demarcation from other areas of social assistance, e.g. medical help, psychotherapy, penitentiary services, youth welfare, self-help. The history of social work in *Germany* is linked to industrialization and its social consequences. Initially, mass poverty was not answered socio-politically, but rather repressively. From 1850 the communal welfare for the poor was reformed, but still charity activities of the churches and private individuals constitute the social support in the 19th century. (Hering, S., Münchmeier, R., 2013)

During this time, the women's movement, which is involved in the field of social work, grew stronger. They are linked to the names *Alice Salomon, Hedwig Heyl and Marie Baum*. One of the endpoints of the activities of the women's movements is the establishment of women's social schools (the first one in Berlin in 1908). It is characteristic of these training centres that these "did not come from educational or scientific circles, ... not from universities or other institutions with social science educational goals, ... but from men and women from social practice." (Ibid., p. 60)

The introduction of the social security systems by the end of the 19th century did not solve all social problems. At the same time, new forms of communal "poor relief" emerged, albeit with legal entitlement and not free from discrimination, mainly with children and young people being the target group for "welfare". On the one hand, the background is to maintain the health of young men (suitability for military service) and the care situation of the children of working mothers. The crisis situation after World War I leads to the "modernization" of welfare and its professionalization. Overdue reforms were carried out. The increase in the number of problem cases caused by the war since the beginning of the war ensures a differentiation in aid (ibid., p.92). The War Welfare Offices provide a legal right to assistance that reduces discrimination.

During this time, the fight against mass misery and the founding of welfare organizations, as well as the development of the fields of action (youth and health care, housing and business welfare and family welfare) fall. In Germany, the historical epoch of the overthrow of the monarchist regime and the founding of the republic led to the establishment of new political rights. The trade unions gain strength, the heyday of the early 1920s is followed by the economic crisis and inflation. This has had an impact on social work. The development of the profession is shaped by the break-in of men into what were previously women dominated field of work. As a result, in addition to the social schools for women, schools for men are now also being established. Women are increasingly being pushed back from responsible positions. The association of social workers fights for ethical standards.

The charities succeed in limiting the increasing state influence by establishing the principle of subsidiarity. The state influence is evident in the legalization of social work. The takeover of power by the National Socialists/Nazis changed social and political life throughout Germany. Especially the so-called *racial hygiene* with the systematic persecution and killing of political opponents and of "anti-social forces" changes also the social work. It is functionalized for the state in the sense of "people care". Social work becomes superfluous because the "people's body" was strengthened and what is degenerate and *"not worth living"* has been weeded out. The education was reformed, schools partly closed and recruited lecturers who are not trained in social work. This throws the quality of training back below the level of 1920. There is occasional resistance to this and was mainly the Jewish teachers who emigrate abroad.

Social work was regulated in the *National Socialist Welfare*, a mass organization in which 12 million people are organized. Both youth care and health care were adapted to the needs of National Socialist/Nazi propaganda. Social work was increasingly *controlling* (housing care) and *selection* (euthanasia program). The selection also permeates youth welfare, in which the genetically healthy young people are brought *up*

> *"in educational homes ... to become useful members of the national community, the inferior, hereditary and anti-social people who are not capable of community and are to be housed and detained in "preservation institutions ".* (P. 201)

Social work after the end of the World War II crisis initiated by the Nazis developed with the rebuilding of the structures of social aid for 11 million refugees. This is followed by the academization of training in West Germany.

Social assistance was also developing in the German Democratic Republic (GDR). Social work in the GDR had to do with almost identical challenges and problems, but took different paths, followed different concepts and was organized differently than in West Germany. Local self-government, federalism and the regional structure were replaced by a centralized structure. Welfare care and education in public institutions were under the direction of the state and the Socialist Unity Party (SED) was responsible. The tasks of youth work were mainly taken over by the Free German Youth (FDJ) founded in 1946. (Koch, 2017) Work with the elderly and people with disabilities was largely taken over by the churches (especially "Inner Mission", as the Protestant church was mainly represented in the GDR). They were also supported with funds from the partner communities in West Germany. For a long time, work with addicts was also in the hands of the churches, and it was only in the last few years of the GDR that state agencies began to take care of it. There was care for the elderly both by the state (through popular solidarity) and by the church. But there was no social work as professionally exercised support for various problem situations in the system of the GDR. In the "socialist society", rather, the problems that led to the emergence and development of social work and social education should be solved. Deviations from "the norm" were considered "anti-social" and were punished with strict educational measures or punishments. There were also a few areas in which carers or educators were active (e.g. raising children). Only in the context of church welfare work existed forms of social work as they were also practiced in Western countries. (Nöthling 2009)

In West Germany 1961 the Federal Social Protection Act (BSHG) was passed, the 1970s were marked by the strengthening of the citizens' movements and the debate about the 'new poverty'. Especially when it comes to the amendment of the Youth Welfare Act (JWG), the costs that are to be made available to youth welfare had been heatedly disputed.

Social work in Germany cannot be understood exclusively as a success story. Rather, they also point to the contradictions with which social work has to deal: between help and control, state aid or private practice organization, between professional requirements and the financial framework.

What social work as a profession, not in the form of individuals, has contributed to the solution of social questions remains open.

3.1. Social work with people with substance use disorder in Germany

The field of addiction help (Klein, 1999) (Laging, 2018) – consisting primarily of the sub-areas of addiction prevention, counseling and therapy – has gained significantly importance for social pedagogues and social workers in recent decades. This is primarily the result of a sharp increase in substance-use-related disorders in the general population, such as problematic consumption and dependence on alcohol, psychotropic medication and illicit drugs, as well as a considerable expansion of the addiction support system since the 1970s. The number of people with alcohol disorder is now estimated at 2.5 million (risky and dangerous consumption of alcohol 8–9 mio., alcohol dependency 1,2 mio.; 1–2 mio. with consumption of illicit substances (mainly with Cannabis and to a certain degree Cocaine consumption; 160.000 Heroin dependents).[14] In addition, there are around 6 million addicted smokers and an unknown number of addicts in the field of non-substance-use-related addictions (e.g. gambling, problematic use of internet).

Due to the strong expansion of the addiction support system since the seventies, more and more client groups have been reached for support measures. In addition, aid measures have developed within the framework of low-threshold services, opioid substitution treatment, and aftercare measures. Addictions have been a dominant social problem for a long time. *Al-*

---

14 Epidemiolgischer Suchtsurvey 2018, Institut für Suchttherapie (IFT) München (epemimiogical addiction survey, Institute for Therapy Research Munich).

coholism as a "social disease" was already discussed in the 1890s. *Alcoholism* gained its great socio-pathological importance through the high proportion of social factors that were involved in the aetiology (Hauschildt, 1995), such as poverty, unemployment, social degradation, debt, homelessness, gender conflicts, and systematic unequal treatment of addicts. The negative effects of alcohol addiction on families, especially children, were discussed very early on.

The overall situation described led to a state-organized *drinkers' welfare* scheme with outpatient and inpatient services even before the World War I, which was then expanded and socially legitimized during the Weimar Republic. After a catastrophic slump during the Nazi regime, it took until the end of the 1960s for addiction support to regain its clear shape in Germany. This renewed development was favoured on one hand by the groundbreaking judgment of the Federal Social Court of June 21, 1968, which recognized alcohol dependency (*alcoholism*) as a disease, on the other hand it was accelerated by the rising drug wave in the course of the 1968 student movement. It is generally recognized that the social professions have made and continue to make a strong contribution to practical addiction support. In addition to doctors and pastors, they were already well represented at the beginning of professional addiction help at the beginning of the 20th century as welfare workers and are still there today as social educators and social workers.

Social work in outpatient addiction support has been part of the support system since the beginning of providing care for addicts/dependents. Although it is often accepted, it still seems unclear in the professional discourse what exactly social work in outpatient addiction support is and how it performs its tasks, especially when dealing with users of legal addictive substances. These activities were reconstructed as part of a qualitative work field analysis. It became clear that social work in outpatient addiction support performs complex activities both on the level of individual contact (micro level) and on the level of networking institutions (meso level) that go well beyond simple addiction history and formal mediation activities. It also became clear, however, that the formal framework does not depict these activities and provides little orientation and security here. Social work professionals need a clearer awareness of their own expertise, and social work concepts must be included more explicitly in organizational structures and quality manuals in order to secure the long-term help potential of social work for clients. (Hansjürgens, 2015)

Drug and addiction help with its areas of addiction prevention, addiction counselling, addiction therapy, and aftercare has become a classic and complex field of social work due to the increase in substance-related disorders such as abuse of alcohol, medication or illicit drugs (e.g. ecstasy, cannabis, methamphetamine), but also other addictive human behaviours (e.g. gambling, eating disorders, shopping addiction) have become significantly more important.

Social work makes a significant contribution to professional addiction support because addiction and dependencies are not only to be treated as illnesses from the perspective of the health system, but must also be accompanied by social offers such as the provision of material help, family work, help for the homeless or community work.

Social workers – with or without addiction therapy qualifications – find a broad field of activities in addiction and drug help, work on different levels according to different concepts and address the different needs and individual problems of clients. In addition to specific specialist knowledge and methodological skills, the development of a clear personal attitude and the discussion of ethical principles in dealing with people with addictions are indispensable and therefore a basic requirement. (Manual, 2016) (DGSAS Competency profile, 2016))

In addition to the work "with the client", the network and cooperative work with social services and other professional groups involved, such as medical doctors, psychologists, pedagogues, psychotherapists, nursing staff or social scientists, is a special component of addiction support. Fixed and sustainable work alliances for the implementation of (early) prevention offers as well as further training or cooperation with job placement institutions are among the core social work areas.

Since addiction is also caused by cultural and social factors, providers and social workers, in addition to their professional role, observe the social situation in our society critically and, as far as they can, influence socio-political decisions. In addition, raising public awareness and educating the public on the subject of addiction and drugs, as well as showing possible help, is a suitable means of actively promoting support for addiction prevention and attracting additional (voluntary) multipliers.

4. Baseline of Social Work development in Central Asia and China

Western models may provide a framework for understanding social work, but different cultural assumptions and social needs may require different models. Healy denotes the difference between global and international social work as *'global... pertaining to or involving the whole world, whereas international can mean... between or among two or more nations...'*. (Healy, 2008: 7)

4.1. Social Work Development in China

The introduction of addiction/drug treatment social work has been possible in Central Asia and China mainly through international funding and collaboration with Western professionals (see Klein, 2008; Michels & Stöver, 2012; Stöver, 2009 for reviews). However, a professional implementation of addiction/drug treatment social work remains very scarce due to lack of funding in both training of social workers as well as development of local harm reduction initiatives. One of the barriers standing in the way of this improvement is stigma. Stigmatization of people who use drugs and their treatment as 'undeserving citizens' is a major issue standing in the way of funding better healthcare and low threshold services for people struggling with addiction (Bernays et al., 2010).

Although organized social work in *China* began more than 30 years ago, social work as profession did not play an explicit role in the grand scheme of "socialist society" until the end of the 20th century (Xiong, Y. & Wang, S., 2007) (Dominelli, 2020). Social work was not considered a necessary profession because as it is in most collectivistic societies and cultures, the neighbourhood committees in the residential districts of the factories took care of all social problems of the population including relationship and family issues, educational and school questions (see also Glazer, 2006). This is also referred to as 'state socialism' (Schwartz, 1994). Needless to say, this often acted as form of 'social control' against 'deviant' and so-called 'anti-social behavior' as a metaphor for any individualistic positioning against the collective idea which most Asian societies are built on. In addition, there is very little record of charities and non-governmental organizations to have had ever functioned in China and that have had attempted to regulate social conflicts in an informal manner. This picture has changed drastically in the last 30 years as the country began to implement professional accreditation of social workers through training, social work degree programs at Universities and professional assessment standards (Xiong, Y. & Wang, S., 2007) (Sherraden et al., 2020). The history of social work education in China is short and started with economic reforms and modernization policy, Chinese social work education revived in the 1980s when four universities were initially approved by the Ministry of Education to establish programs on 'Social Work and

Management'—designed to train social work students.[15] [16][17]With the expansion of social work schools, the China Association for Social Work Education (CASWE) has played a significant role in leading and promoting professional social work training and has had a profound influence both on formalizing the curriculum and improving the quality of social work teaching. This development is evident in China's new commitment goal to Middle-to-long Term Development Plan for Social Work Professionals 2011–2020 (Ministry of Civil Affairs PRC, 2012). Governmental action is highly regarded as a legitimate intervening role of the state in resolving social and personal conflicts. Social work is subordinate to it by definition: Angelina Yuen-Tsang – one of the leading theorists of social work in China – defines this as a specific character of social work in PR China in that the profession is often funded inside the state agencies (Yuen-Tsang et al., 2016). This means that workers are mostly state employees who work within government-compliant bureaucracy. The voluntary sector of social work, she adds, is yet in its budding stages (Yuen-Tsang et al., 2016: 177). The curriculum of the China Association of Social Work provides an "[e]ducation model which emphasizes theory-practice integration, critical reflection, action learning, culturally sensitive practice and commitment to social change and development" (Yuen-Tsang et al., 2016: 178).

> *"In perspective, it is important to observe how the interaction process between administrative social work and social work in the western sense works. Scientists and practitioners of social work, both from Germany and China, can actively participate in this process by e.g. train staff and conduct research. It is precisely at this point that I see the potential intersection between China and Germany in the context of the cooperation. When it comes to staff training for university teachers, practitioners or volunteers, the focus may be on the transfer of knowledge about methods and work techniques."* (Zhang, W., 2009; 112)

---

15 Tom Chan Kam Tong, David Ip Fu Keung & Ava Lau Siu Mei (2009) Social work professionalization in China: the case of Shenzhen, China Journal of Social Work, 2:2, 85-94, DOI: 10.1080/17525090902992222
16 Chan K.L., Chan C. (2005): Chinese culture, social work education and research; Journal of International So-cial Work; July 1
17 Bin, X. (2009) The Future for Rural Social Work In China, Rural Society, 19:4, 280- 282, DOI: 10.5172/rsj.351.19.4.280

4.2. Social Work Development in Central Asia

4.2.1. Social Work Development in Kazakhstan

In the post-soviet region and specifically Central Asia, social work has even a more recent history as the professionalization of this discipline is only beginning now. Unlike China, in Central Asia reliance of social work services on a centralized government system has not been the dominant model of social work. In fact, the available few research studies show that post-Soviet legacy of denial of 'social diseases' such as addiction, HIV/AIDS has been a dominant approach in denying professional services to people of such marginalized cohorts (Tulchinsky & Varavikova, 1996). "In response to the social problems in *Kazakhstan*, various governmental and non-governmental institutions rendered services to vulnerable people. However, before the development of nongovernmental organizations (NGOs) in the 1990s, many social issues, such as alcohol and drug dependence, were mainly responded to with a medical intervention (Fleming et al., n.d.), and little attention was given to working with people at individual and interpersonal levels." (Grebneva, I., 2006; 819) In Kazakhstan, the official education of social work began in early 2000s and almost simultaneously in 20 Universities across the country, including three in the capital city Astana (Zinovieva & Naumova, 2017). Treated as a form of social communication skill and defined as a social policy strategy, the current social work curricula in Kazakhstan serves two main aims: 1) to teach students methods of communicating between state institutions and clientele in medical institutions, kindergartens, schools, and care for disabled people and 2) to work closely with the local offices of Labor, Employment and Social Protection of Astana city on the employment of social work course graduates (Zinovieva & Naumova, 2017). Treated as a form of social communication skill and defined as a social policy strategy, the current social work curricula in Kazakhstan serves two main aims: 1) to teach students methods of communicating between state institutions and clientele in medical institutions, kindergartens, schools, and care for disabled people and 2) to work closely with the local offices of Labour, Employment and Social Protection of Astana city on the employment of social work course graduates (Zinovieva & Naumova, 2017). In the InBeAIDS report (In BeAids 2020, p58 ff) it was mentioned that in Kazakhstan when it comes to the needs of the client, more medical worker than specialists in social work are involved, the medical model of care is dominant. The role of a social worker is not stable and is often dependent on factors that are directly independent of him, such as the degree of participation in a project, the presence of a social worker's position in a project, etc., avail-able information about social support methods. People living with HIV/AIDS (PLHIV) are generally more accessible for psychological support, since the psychologist's vacancies in medical organizations had been reduced and psychosocial support is provided. But the psychologists do not have the opportunity to engage in broader is-sues, such as social assistance of the client, linking with other sectors, organizing cross-sectoral work (such as with the families involved). Stigma is still existing in the society towards people living with HIV, also by the attitude of medical staff, so that PLHIV feel not confident, so it is uncomfortable speaking about their illness, diagnosis during medical consultations. In Kazakhstan social work on drug addiction and HIV is emerging, but quite slowly. It is mostly done by local NGOs, organized though outreach workers, trained by these NGOs. They know about the problem from an *inside perspective*. They also provide information for NGOs, decision- and policy makers feel the situation and have knowledge in terms of regulation and further implication to policy with an enhanced understanding of the current situation. Today in Kazakhstan there is a difficult situation with the professionalization of social work. More than 20 universities have licenses to pro-vide bachelor degrees in Social work. [18] There are several factors that inhibit its development: – Even if a position of a social work specialist is present in a medical institution, the functions of this specialist are not transparent and are often performed by specialists with medical education, that's why the medical aspect of the work prevails. Another factor is the vulnerability of the profession itself due to its young history in the country. The first branches of social work were opened about 20 years, ago, but have not yet received their sustainability in the

---

18 18 Yessimova, D. (Eurasian National University, Nur-Sul- tan, Kazakhstan), Ab-dykalykova, Zh. (National Alliance of Professional Social Workers, Almaty, Kazakhstan) (2020): Social Work in Kazakhstan. Educational work for «Improvement of social work curriculum social work at the national level» Year: April 2017- May 2018. One of the tasks – elaboration of manuals for in-service level workers 1) The main stages of Case-management in work with families; 2) Plan to work with family; 3) Supervision in Social Work among package of 8 modules. Elaboration of self-assessment tool to manage the content in SW education Organization Winter School by Social Work specialty among 10 KZ universities. « Improvement of Social work curriculum at the national level» project by UNICEF and Eurasian National University. Developing and conducting trainings of home visiting for Kyzylorda region (trainings by UNICEF package modules for Home visiting. Supervision of the policlinic teams in pilot policlinics of Kyzylorda region. Developed and conducted ToT training for high medical colleagues from 8 regions of Kazakhstan (October 2017, Burabay).

country. The first doctoral program in social work, PhD, was opened in 2006 at Al-Farabi Kazakh National University in collaboration with the D. Brown School of Social Work, Missouri, USA (Grebneva, 2006). This barrier exacerbates the advocacy of social work as an academic discipline and profession. So far there are no faculties and departments of social work, it is always a related discipline with other disciplines in the department (such as pedagogic or psychology). This makes it difficult to develop separate, specialized education tools for maintenance, for example, for working with PLHIV. The third fac-tor, one of the most serious barriers, is the low salary of social work professionals working in governmental institutions for social support. This factor impedes the awareness of families, children, clients about the possibilities of social support from the state. In a survey conducted within the InBeAIDS study in 2018 on the experiences of both clients as well as experts working in the field, it was reflected in the respondents' answers that they did not know where their social protection centres are located in the city or they did not be aware of the civil rights of the clients and what kind of help they can receive, or the clients had been cautious to public their HIV status because they are afraid of prejudices or stigmatization. Thus, there is low confidence in specialists due to stigma (InBeAIDS, p 58). There is a need for a law on the status of a social worker and awareness of social work. A revision and analysis of the need for specialists in social work is now on the political agenda; a *Social Code* law is in preparation which could help to enrich and revise the current main Law in Special Social Services from 2009, which is not responding to the current situation of social work mentioned above. Social work shall be adapted to the international definition (IFSW, 2000) and with the inclusion of the concepts of «case management», «work with people on high risk», supervision, in–depth assessment-intervention, in-dividual family development plan etc.; also to de-fine a professional approach in the areas of health care the penitentiary system, probation, educational institutes. It is necessary to consolidate a revealing approach to client needs rather than a declarative one. It is also needed to prepare programs at the level of professional development for practical social workers in the direction of assessment of psycho-social interventions for each individual case to develop an effective client support system. It is also needed to develop programs educating social workers in the field of narcology and HIV/AIDS, for (out-reach) social workers of NGOs, as well as for volunteers and also for the penitentiary system. There are also needs for trainings in case management technology based on the empowerment approach. Developing of skills in assessing one`s own work is also needed and programs with focus on employment. The Ministry of La-bour and Social Protection of population of the Republic of Kazakhstan held a virtually an *Inter-national Social Workers Online Forum* on August 12, 2020. The event was attended by about 500 people, including social workers of Kazakhstan, representatives of international organizations, non-governmental sector and government agencies. Experts from Russia, the USA, Israel, Bulgaria, Georgia and Kyrgyzstan made presentations. [19] There had been very interesting presentations such as "Conceptual approaches for the development of social work in Kazakh-stan" by the Kazakh Vice-Minister Aukenov Muratovich; a "Presentation of the program of testing and training of social workers in 2020" by Raisova Fazylovna, the Director of the National Resource Center for Social Work); an "Overview of the main directions of development and practice of social work in Kyrgyzstan" by Orozova Rakhat (Kyrgyzstan) of the Master of Social Work and Social Management of the University of Manchester; with a Speech of Ongarbaev Anuarovich, the Vice-rector for educational and methodological work of ENU named after L.N.Gumilyov, on the topic: "Education in the field of social work in higher education: challenges and next steps» or a speech of Dr. Timo-thy Hunt, Researcher at Columbia University on the topic: "Assessment of educational and training needs of social workers employees: results of Columbia University's initial report". Also Aysel Sultan, from the Institute of Addiction Re-search at the Frankfurt University of Applied Sciences in Germany, could present the international project "SOLID" (Germany, China, Kazakhstan, Kyrgyzstan, Uzbekistan) on the topic: "Strengthening the social work of NGOs. Work with HIV and drug addicts, convicts". This indicates the fast growing development of Social Work education and the commitment of the Kazakh government on this issue. [20] The Director of the National Resource Center for Social Work, Lira Raisova, presented the testing system for social workers to improve the quality of the pro-vision of special social services. She noted that a social worker who does not score a threshold score will receive additional training, and a low score will not be a reason for dismissal. Testing will consist of questions on the legislation of the Republic of Kazakhstan and ethics of social work, as well as practical tasks.

---

19 19 III online forum of social workers (III онлайн-форум соцработников); Department for the coordination of em- ployment and social programs of the Kyzylorda region August 13, 2020 III онлайн-форум соцработников (www.gov.kz).

20 20 Program of the *International Social Workers Online Forum*, Nur Sultan, August 2020

4.2.2 Social Work Development in Kyrgyzstan

In the *Kyrgyz Republic* the establishment of a Social Work Department at the Bishkek Humanitarian University started in 1994, in 1998 on an initiative of the Association of Social Workers social work was registered as a profession by the Ministry of Labour and Social Development. (Sheripkanova, 2020). At the beginning, the his-tory of social work in Kyrgyzstan is describing precisely the cultural and historical features of the formation of ideas of social work in Kyrgyz society. [21] *Nurgul Musaeva* describes this in her survey *"Social work as an object of philosophical analysis"*, where all these issues had been reflected, the cultural and traditional features of the system of mutual assistance in the Kyrgyz society. (Musaeva, 2012) [22]

> *"Familiarity with the rich world experience is significant for our social work and borrowing some of his positive achievements. But, the national model of social work, which is being formed in Kyrgyzstan, can be effective only while maintaining its distinctive features, national and cultural traditions. Subjects of social works should be based on historical and spiritual heritage and use national and cultural levers in overcoming social difficulties. At the same time, the ideological guidelines of Kyrgyz thinkers can be a kind of spiritual basis for the formation of the Kyrgyz social work models."* (Musaeva, 2012)

What caused the need for the training of professional social workers, the development of social work as a type of social activity and academic discipline in Kyrgyzstan? It was facilitated by several factors: the inten-

---

21 See: *Umetalieva C., Topchubekova (2017): Cultural Approach to the problem – study of ethnogenesis of Kyrgyz (УМЕТАЛИЕВА-БАЯЛИЕВА ЧЫНАР ТОПЧУБЕКОВНА: КУЛЬТУРОЛОГИЧЕСКИЙ ПОДХОД К ПРОБЛЕМЕ ИЗУЧЕНИЯ ЭТНОГЕНЕЗА КЫРГЫЗОВ).*
   It must be assumed that intonational- figurative thinking in humans appeared earlier than rational-logical thinking. Thus, musical thinking occupies an intermediate position between the two main signaling systems, being a manifestation of the subconscious. How this is influencing the conceptualization of societal behaviour including social work might be discussed.
22 In another article Nurgul Musaeva reveals the influence of national traditions on the formation of the psychology of the Kyrgyz people. It also highlights the psychological significance of such traditions. See: Musaeva, N. (2017): Na- tional traditions as a factor of formation of the social char- acter of the Kyrgyz people (Н.К. Мусаева, Национальные традиции как фактор формирования социального характера кыргызского народа); In: Interactive Science, 3(13) 2017, p.101 – 103 (Интеракт-ивная наука | 3 (13) • 2017) DOI 10.21661/r-118248

sive ideological and socio-political transformations affecting all spheres of public life, social difficulties that developed during the transition period, political and economic instability, growing social differentiation, poverty, exacerbation of migration problems caused by mass unemployment, and much more. [23] Therefore, in order to stabilize the standard of living in the Republic of Kyrgyzstan, it became necessary to move from public administration to professional social work and begin to build a fundamentally new social policy, which should be based on social protection and support for people in difficult life situations. In addition to state social institutions, innovative methods and approaches of social work had been implemented NGOs. *Musaeva* mentioned, that on June 5, 2008 at Issyk-Kul a scientific-practical conference *"Intensification of cooperation of the CIS member states in solving social problems"* of mutual interest was held. The conference was attended by representatives of the CIS countries: Azerbaijan, Armenia, Belarus, Kazakhstan, Russian Federation, Tajikistan, Uzbekistan. During the conference, the geography of mutual interests of all CIS countries in solving social problems had been presented, the existing problems of all CIS countries had been reflected and international-level measures had been identified in enhancing cooperation for their solution. Much attention had also been paid to the formation of the foundations of a scientific approach to the problem of overcoming poverty. A close relationship had been established between the Bishkek State University (BSU) and foreign universities from Sweden, USA and Russia. Representatives of these universities conducted lectures, practical classes, round tables, seminars, trainings for students and teachers of Bishkek university. [24] The organizational-practical,

---

23 „ *Social work in Kyrgyz society has a rich history development. Its genesis and developmental evolution are closely related to the nomadic way life, social norms and principles, national and cultural values, worldview and philosophy of the people. Nomadic community and generic relations were peculiar subjects, which provided social and physical security, ethnic identification and socialization of the individual in society. Fundamentals of Social Ideas works were laid in oral folk art, socially oriented ethno-national traditions, customs and beliefs of the Kyrgyz people, which embody the principles of humanism, unity and helping each other in difficult situations. We believe that reliance on centuries-old life experience of gen-erations, respect for cultural traditions, preservation of the system of values developed over the centuries greatly enriched the content of modern social work, would help create Kyrgyz national model of social work.*" (Musaeva, 2012, Conclusion).

24 It is mentioned on the website of the Association of Social workers of the Kyrgyz Republic (ASWKR) organized project such as "Training/development of social work with families and children at risk in Kyrgyzstan" from 2002 – 2009 with the support of the Swedish Agency for International Cooperation or a joint partnership with the Association of Social Workers of Denmark already in 1998 as well as

theoretical-methodological and legislative-legal bases of social work have been fixed, the process of training and retraining of personnel is being improved, taking into account innovative forms and methods of teaching. It is also important to mention the Bishkek-2018 International Conference "The Role of Civil Society /NGO/Self-Help and Social Work in Drug Addiction and Infectious Disease Prevention among Injecting Drug Users".[25] The results shall be taken into account. By such international cooperation, the mechanism and system of social protection and social services for the population are being improved. Institutions of social protection have been established at all levels, from district to republican, in order to re-duce poverty, develop social protection, and rendering assistance to vulnerable parts of the population. Social workers in Kyrgyzstan were first brought into statutory professional regulation in 2012, and standards of conduct and pratice for the profession had been implemented. A register of professionals exists who meet the standards. It shall ensure high standards of education for social workers, including a code of ethics of social workers. There are several accredited institutions for training of social work specialists, such as the Kyrgyz National University (Bachelor's degree, 4 years); the Bishkek State (former Humanitarian) University (Bachelor's and Master's degree); the Osh State University (Bachelor's degree, 4 years); the Zhalalabad University (Bachelor's degree, 4 years); the Pedagogical University named after I. Arabaev (Bachelor's and Master's degree); the Institute of Social Development and Entrepreneur- ship(Bachelor's degree, 4 years) and the Inter- national University of Kyrgyzstan (Bachelor's and Master's degree).

This has been implemented with the support of foreign partners on the development of both practical social work and the development of professionalization of social work. This influence was enormous. Various

---

the project "Development of Occupational Therapy in Kyrgyzstan" in 1999 with the support of the Russian-Euro-pean- Union. Since 2009, the Kyrgyz NGO have been collaborating with the Danish NGO "European House" (Det Europiske Hus or TEH). The two NGOs are working closely together to continue integrating disadvantaged members of society and to create greater opportunities for people living in various Kyrgyz government institutions. They did so, working both in disciplines and sectors. This included not only workshops for social workers, but also cross-sectoral workshops in which parent associations, small NGOs, local municipalities, businesses, students and, above all, social assistance recipients would participate in discussions and give their own results and share their experiences. All theoretical work has led to three social enterprises, primarily in the country, which will be based in public institutions. http://aswkr.tilda.ws/.

25 See at the website of the Association of Social workers of the Kyrgyz Republic

assistance had been provided. Local civil society organizations had been and are acting as implementers of professional development trainings for social workers and inter- national organizations mainly act as donors and fund various social work-related trainings, but there is established also a good cooperation be- tween Kyrgyz universities and the Ministry of Social Development in terms of the development of social work in general. [26] But there are still several challenges of social work education in Kyrgyzstan, such as a gap between education, training and practice application; a high turnover (low wages, low status of social work in the country); a lack of professional support and guidance of social work specialists in state and municipal organizations/supervision; a lack of the third cycle of education in social work in Kyrgyzstan; the professional community is not commissioned to establish the standards [27]; the absence of one centralized educational institution which could examine the knowledge and skills of social workers and provide licensing and further professional career development or in-service training for state and municipal social workers without specific social work education. Universities, non-profit organizations and state social institutions closely cooperate to fill the gap in social work education, training and practice application; the Social Work Alumni Association of the Kyrgyz Republic shall develop structured professional development courses for social workers on relevant topics[28] , as a research centre/think tank). Social work education should adapt a business model and develop a leader- ship for management.[29] But there also several achievements of Social Worker education in Kyrgyzstan, such as Guidelines on status of a social worker developed by Ministry of Labour and Social Development of the Kyrgyz Republic in December 2017 (under

---

26 . See the website of the Bishkek State University about International Cooperation: Международные связи – Бишкекский Государственный Университет им. К. Карасаева (bhu.kg).

27 There is really no professional standard for social work. This should be developed by practitioners. The state standard of higher professional education is of course available, but updates are necessary

28 But this organization exists only formally, only a few events had been held, but neither the practicing social workers in the regions nor universities know anything about them.

29 It is important to emphasize the role of the Association of Social Workers of the Kyrgyz Republic. Its role is enor-mous in the development of social work and in the opening of the specialty "Social work". Thanks to the initiative of this Association, in 1994 the first enrollment of students for this new profession was carried out. Keeping in touch with foreign universities, the association helped to obtain books, programs, manuals, magazines and articles on social work.

consideration); outsourcing of state social services (crisis shelters, training of foster families, care for children with disability etc.); an increased under-standing of social work as a profession among the general public and sta-ble wages for social workers working in state and municipal institutions (local self-governance, schools).

4.2.3 Social Work Development in Tajikistan

In *Tajikistan*, the commencement of social work education also coincided to early 2000s. A social work educator from UK – Alison McInnes – was among the first Western academics who kicked off the development agen-da for social work education in Tajikistan in 2008. (McInnes, A., 2012)

The sociality of the state of Tajikistan is enshrined in its Constitution. The National Development Strategy of the country for the period up to 2030 lists among the main challenges the in-sufficient effectiveness of social services provided to vulnerable social groups, such as per-sons with disabilities and senior citizens, children from poor families, mothers caring for children with disabilities, pensioners and low-in-come families. [30] The process of developing social work as one of the main directions of state social policy in Tajikistan is taking place in the context of the formation of a market economy and the formation of a national concept of social protection. Practice shows that the staffing of this process, being a key component of it, is becoming a top priority in the sphere of science, edu-cation and training. In other words, social work as a professional activity as well as the current state policy of the country in the field of social protection of the population requires a level of qualification and compe-tence of social workers that is appropriate to the rather difficult state and public tasks. In this context, social work as a new profession in Tajikistan began to develop relatively recently – in the early 2000s, due to the need to overcome the negative effects of the civil war and the cataclysmic trans-formation of socio-economic relations. At the same time, in some post-So-viet countries the professionalization of social work began about 10 years earlier. In 2002 there were more than 3,000 specialists working in social protection, many of whom had no professional training in social work (doctors, educators, psychologists, sociologists, etc.). The developing social

---

30 National Development Strategy of the Republic of Tajikistan until 2030// Resolu-tion of the Majlisi Oli of the Re-public of Tajikistan, December 1, 2016, No. 636. p. 30–31.

work, first and foremost, needed qualified specialists. The formation and development of social work as a profession was largely due to the work of international NGOs. From September 2002 to February 2004, ORA International [31] organized the first six-month course in Dushanbe to train social workers.[32][33][] The courses were taught by experienced professors from

---

31 is a Christian aid organization that has been committed to children and families in need since 1981 and is active in ten countries and ensures that children are adequately fed, adequately clothed, have medical care and can go to school regularly; financially supported by the German Federal Ministry of Economic Development and International Cooperation (BMZ)32 The course program included theoretical foundations of social work practice: introduction to the specialty, general and family psychology, personality development, basics of communication, sociology, professional ethics of a social worker, record keeping in social work, human rights, children's rights, current national legislation on social work, social work with family, social work with community, social work with the disabled, social work in school, etc.33 Zevarov H., Rasulov O. (2019): Development of social work in pro-Soviet states/ Tutorial. Dushanbe

34 The course consisted of 8 modules of 14 days each: "Comparative Social Policy", "Contemporary Theories of Social Work", "Methods of Research and Evaluation in Social Work", "Social Work with Family and Couples", "Social Work with People with Disabilities", "Social Work with Children in Difficult Life Situation", "Social Work with Teenagers". Of the 35 students who attended the courses, 14 graduated with a degree from Stockholm University and laid the foundation for the development of academic education in social work

28 see Zevarov H., Rasulov; ibidem

29 Raimdodov U. (2016): Training of social workers in Tajikistan // Labour relations and social protection of the population: Mater of the republican scientific and practical conference, Dushanbe, 2006; Raimdodova, M. U. Problems and prospects of staff resources of social work in Tajiki-stan / M. U. Raimdodova M.U., Nevarov A.A. Text: immediate // Aktual. – Text: Immediate // Actual issues of mod-ern pedagogy: Proceedings of the VIII International Scientific Conference. (Samara, March 2016). -Samara: LLC "Publishing house ASGARD", p. 303–306.: https://moluch.ru/conf/ped/archive/188/9947/ (access date: 23.06.2020)

30 Currently, in the frame of Caritas Germany the project is financed by the Federal Ministry of Economic Development and International Cooperation (BMZ), professionals in the field of social work are also being trained in Khorog and Kulyab State Universities

32 The course program included theoretical foundations of social work practice: introduction to the specialty, general and family psychology, personality development, basics of communication, sociology, professional ethics of a social worker, record keeping in social work, human rights, chil-dren's rights, current national legislation on social work, social work with family, social work with community, social work with the disabled, social work in school, etc.

33 Zevarov H., Rasulov O. (2019): Development of social work in pro-Soviet states/ Tutorial. Dushanbe

universities in New Zealand, Germany and Scotland. The course consisted
of theoretical (three months) and practical (three months) parts. In 2004–
2006, the project "Development of Aca-demic Capacity in Social Work"
was implemented under the Ministry of Labour and Social Protection of
the Republic of Tajikistan. With the support of UNICEF, social work professors from Stockholm University conducted a master's course for social
work teachers. [34][From 2002–2006, within the framework of the Asian
Development Bank project, more than 2,000 social workers were trained
under programs: "Computerization of the Social Sector", "Personification
of Social Assistance and Services", and "Banking Services for Retirees".
The implementation of this project contributed to the reform of the social
sector in our country[35] []. As part of a European Union project in 2007,
the organization *Hilfswerk (Austria)* created the first day-care rehabilitation
centres for children with disabilities and a day-centres for the elderly.[36]
[] From 2008–2010, the *Area Social Service Centres for the Elderly* were
opened in three districts with funding from the EU and Caritas Germany.
Social workers for the social centres were trained in the framework of the
projects, as there was still a shortage of social work specialists. In 2008,
the Government of the Republic of Tajikistan instructed the Ministries
of Education and Economy to begin training social work specialists at
the Tajik National University (TNU) and other educational institutions.
In September 2008, the TNU Faculty of Economics began training social
workers with higher education at full-time and part-time departments[37]]
In 2008, the State Institution *"Centre for Adult Education of Tajikistan"*

---

34 The course consisted of 8 modules of 14 days each: "Comparative Social Policy", "Contemporary Theories of Social Work", "Methods of Research and Evaluation in So-cial Work", "Social Work with Family and Couples", "Social Work
with People with Disabilities", "Social Work with Chil-dren in Difficult Life
Situation", "Social Work with Teenagers". Of the 35 students who attended the
courses, 14 graduated with a degree from Stockholm University and laid the
foundation for the development of academic edu-cation in social work
35 see Zevarov H., Rasulov; ibidem
36 Raimdodov U. (2016): Training of social workers in Ta-jikistan // Labour relations and social protection of the pop-ulation: Mater of the republican scientific
and practical con-ference, Dushanbe, 2006; Raimdodova, M. U. Problems and
prospects of staff resources of social work in Tajiki-stan / M. U. Raimdodova
M.U., Nevarov A.A. Text: imme-diate // Aktual. - Text: Immediate // Actual issues
of mod-ern pedagogy: Proceedings of the VIII International Scien-tific Conference. (Samara, March 2016). -Samara: LLC "Publishing house ASGARD", p.
303-306.: https://moluch.ru/conf/ped/archive/188/9947/ (access date: 23.06.2020)
37 Currently, in the frame of Caritas Germany the project is financed by the Federal
Ministry of Economic Develop-ment and International Cooperation (BMZ), pro-

was established under the Ministry of Labour and Social Protection of the Republic of Tajikistan. Today it has branches in more than 30 towns and districts of the republic. In 2009, the list of professions included the working profession of "social worker assistant" and short-term training courses were organized38The branch of Caritas Germany Association in Tajikistan, within the framework of the project "Strengthening vocational training in rehabilitation at community level and structures established earlier in Tajikistan" (2018–2020) has implemented a number of activities to further professionalize social work. For example, in 2019, professional standards and curricula for social work professions for all three levels of professional education in the country were developed and approved by the relevant state authorities.39 In 2012, graduates of the fellowship programs of these institutions, together with TNU professors, organized the Association of Professional Social Workers of Tajikistan, which is a member of the International Association of Social Workers. Members of the Association developed the "Code of Ethics of a Social Worker" as well as textbooks in the national language: "Introduction to Social Work", "Social Work with the Family", and "Manual for Social Workers". The process of professionalization of social work in Tajikistan continues.

In *Uzbekistan*, giving help to neighbors, mercy and charity have always been intrinsic values since ancient times, as a "core of ancient national values, traditions and customs" (Ganieva, M. & Kim L., 2010). According to practical necessity for support of various groups of the population in need are described as matters of new global and regional economic challenges which apply "the methods of social assistance accumulated over centuries of social history". Ganieva describes the historical system as follows: "Social-tribal and household help, mutual aid and protection within the kinship systems (the concept of 'kin' here standing for a variety of immediate and wider family systems), the family, and the community were its basic organic forms in the historical context. The solidarity and mutual ties of the members of the family and wider family structures were naturally expressed in the kin-based organization of the population." The Islamic period in the history of people of Central Asia continued and diversified the participation by the clergy in social life, even in Soviet times. (Fariev, 2007). The policy of help to vulnerable groups has been carried on since gaining sovereignty, and this applies above all to low-income families, orphans and children without parental care, people with disabil-

---

fessionals in the field of social work are also being trained in Khorog and Kulyab State Universities

ities, and some others who receive certain financial subsidies and other benefits, labor migrants and their families and now also for drug dependent people. This type of social welfare is distributed by the district-based social security departments ("sobès") and institutions of local government, the "mahalla's". Social work as an academic discipline is a systematized approach based on scientific foundations, taught in accordance with the specialization of the institution. Social work students get to master various theoretical knowledge and techniques enabling the interaction between social worker and client, between people in need and the community. The system of education in this area must be a combination of theoretical and practical elements. The main goal of education is acquisition of knowledge, practical skills and techniques corresponding to basic requirements of training of the specialist in social work. Within a short period of time after beginning the process of institutionalization of social work in Uzbekistan, within the system of higher education one can see the trend of expansion of the network of universities, colleges, and specialized re-training courses engaged in training of personnel for the social sphere.

In all Central Asian countries, social work and training for social work are relatively new phenomena of social development, which require a new way of dealing with social problems of a community in the new development. This is all the more true when dealing with problems related to the consumption of psychoactive substances, because two behavioral mechanisms still dominate these developments: on the one hand, the users are stigmatized insofar as they are using illicit substances – even if their use in Central Asia has a long history. On the other hand there are applications, especially for opiates, and medical treatment systems and, at most, psychotherapeutic interventions dominate. Social work is largely not yet established in this field and there are no specific application standards, fields of work or training curricula. That will be the exciting future task in the development of social work.

5. Conclusion: The key issues for Social Work with drugs users and people living with HIV and AIDS in Central Asia and China

Today in Central Asian countries, such as Kazakhstan, the Kyrgyz Republic, Uzbekistan and Tajikistan [40][38], but also in PR China there is a

---

38 40 Prevention of infectious diseases and treatment of HIV / AIDS and hepatitis among injecting drug users in Central Asia and the contribution of social work

difficult situation regarding the professionnalization of social work as a profession with the focus on working with dependent people. There are several factors that inhibit its development: 1) even if the vacancy of a social work specialist is present in a medical institution, the functions of a specialist is not transparent, it is often per-formed by specialists with medical education. Therefore, the medical aspect of the work with drug users and people living with HIV/AIDS and drug addiction prevails. 2) the vulnerability of the profession itself due to its young history in these regions. The first branches of social work were opened about 20 – 30 years ago, but have not yet received their sustainability in the countries. No doctoral pro-grams in social work are existing. [41][39] This barrier exacerbates the advocacy of social work as an academic discipline and profession [42].[40] So far there are no or few faculties and departments of social work in Central Asia and none for social work with drug users, it is always a related discipline with other disciplines in the paedagogique or psychological departments. This makes it difficult to develop separate, specialized technologies for maintenance, for example, for working with drug users and PLHIV. 3) One of the most serious barriers, is the low salary of social work professionals working in governmental institutions for social support. This factor impedes the awareness of families, children, clients about the possibilities of social support from the state. These people are shy of their status with drug use and HIV and don't apply because they are afraid of prejudices or stigmatization. Thus, there is low confidence in specialists due to stigma.

What can social work do? A social worker can provide the following services to people from key populations: 1. Implementation of case management. The activities of social workers are carried out on the basis of case management. Depending on the needs of key groups and their specific needs, a social support program should be developed. The result of social support is to improve the quality of life of clients. Social support in-

---

to the services for drug using people (InBeAIDS) Frankfurt am Main/Ger-many, Bishkek/Kyrgyz Republic March 2020.

39   41 With regard to doctoral studies, there is an initiative for developing these opportunities to defend PhD theses. 3 universities of the Kyrgyz Republic have begun to work on the opening of dissertation councils for doctoral studies. The Government approved regulations for awarding PhD qualifications. More details https://bilim.akipress.org/ru/news:1668827/?f=cp; https://bilim.akipress.org/ru/n ews:1668827?place=share-fab Постановление Правительства КР от 18 сентября 2020 года №491 Об одобрении Национальной рамки квалификаций https://www .gov.kg/ru/npa/s/2709.

40   42 That`s why the SOLID exceed program wants to change this situation.

volves compliance with such principles of work as: an individual approach, comprehensiveness, confidentiality, voluntariness, tolerance and inter- disciplinarity. 2. An interdisciplinary approach and teamwork helps to increase the efficiency and quality of the services provided. This approach defines emergency intervention, diagnostics and discussion of the case, the coordination of the actions of experts, responsibility and activity aimed at solving problems and the effectiveness of work algorithms. Much attention is paid to establishing contact between specialists and clients. 3. According to social and outreach workers, the technology of social work with key population groups should be focused on personality change and reducing the degree of behavioural risks. 4. The fight against stigma. Social workers can play an important role in changing public opinion, creating tolerance for HIV-positive people in society, as well as mobilizing and activating people involved in the problem. This can be carried out with the help of high quality information campaigns targeted at different target groups, involving the media, demonstrating good practices in integrating people living with HIV, individual and group social work to develop people's potential, etc. 5. The protection of the rights and interests of citizens is an important area, which can be man-ifested in different ways: developing policies, lobbying, raising public awareness, public education, conducting campaigns, creating alliances, etc. Social workers provide advisory assistance to clients in case of loss of documents, restoration and paperwork, playing an important connecting and intermediary function between the client and the relevant authorities. 6. The provision of social services and humanitarian assistance (providing material assistance, providing services of crisis centres, shelters for victims of violence), assistance in finding employment (vocational training, retraining and advanced training of unemployed citizens, providing information about employment opportunities, employment). 6. The provision of social services and humanitarian assistance (providing material assistance, providing services of crisis centres, shelters for victims of violence), assistance in finding employment (vocational training, retraining and advanced training of unemployed citizens, providing information about employment opportunities, employment).

6. *The new programme: Social work and strengthening of NGOs in development co-operation to treat drug addiction*

In the course of CADAP VI, contacts were made to 3 Central Asian universities that train social workers (as being done at the Frankfurt University). Existing contacts have been expanded into an university partnership with several universities in Central Asia and China, [43] with a jointly developed research program on the influence of social work on the prevention and treatment of drug / opioid addiction as well as the development of study programs / training curricula for social work with drug-consuming and addicted people (who also live with HIV/AIDS, and/or hepatitis) and the exchange of German and Central Asian scientists and students for research stays in Frankfurt / M. and Central Asia. The English skills of the local scientists are also to be pro-moted, since communication so far has been carried out almost exclusively in Russian and European and international research literature in English is only communicated incompletely. It is also being considered to implement the program in cooperation with the Shanghai Mental Health Center and The Shanghai Jiaotong University. [44][4142] The program is also part of the "EU – Central Asia Strategy" (the European Union has re-leased an update, moving from a "strategy for a

---

41 43 with Bishkek State University, Department of Social Work and Practical Psychology (Bishkek, Kyrgyzstan); Eurasian National University Gumilyov, Department of Sociology (Astana / Nur-Sultan, Kazakhstan); the Bukhara State Medical Institute in cooperation with the Human Re-search and Development Center (Inson Tadqiqoti va Taraqqiyoti Markazi) (Bukhara, Uzbekistan) and the Mental Health Centre in cooperation with Jiao Tong University School of Medicine (Shanghai, PR China. In 2021 also the Russian-Tajik-Slavonic-University (RTSU) in Dushanbe, Tajikistan, joined the project.

42 44 At the Shanghai East China University of Science and Technology (ECUST), Faculty of Social Work at the Soci-ological Institute, it was held an international conference on social work in 2007 with representatives of the Frankfurt University of Applied Sciences.[Michels I.I. (2007): International Conference on" Knowledge, Policy and Ser-vice: A Dialogue Between East and West on Social Work" organized by the East China University of Science & Technology und der Shanghai Normal University on 28th and 29th of October in Shanghai. Internal Report]. Dr. Michels (at that time as visiting professor, on leave by the Federal Ministry of Health, Berlin) conducted as well a series of lectures in 2007 as a visiting professor on social work with drug users. *"I discussed the role of psycho-social sup-port in treatment of (drug) addiction and gave a brief overview on the counseling process, the range of social support systems and methods. I underlined the im-portance of vocational training for the process of recovery and the necessary involvement of the society. The students had been very much interested in learning about these experiences and to adapt them to the specific cultural and social conditions of the Chinese Society. We dis-cussed all these issues and the students asked a lot of questions about the European experiences and how to implement these experiences into the Chinese setting. The lectures broadened the intercultural exchange of experiences and models of the role and work of social workers in modern societies."* Michels I.I. (2007): *"Models of social work with drug users in Europe"*. Lectures at the East China University of Science & Technology (ECUST) Department of Social Work Institute of Applied Sociology in cooperation with Fan Zhihai Fan and Dr. Xuesong He; In-ternal Report, Shanghai June 1st.

new partnership" to "new opportunities for a stronger partnership." published in July 2019 and supported by the German Federal Govern-ment. The objectives of the Sustainable Development Goals (SDG 2030) should serve as a benchmark in the planned program, in particular *Goal: 3 Health and Wellbeing "Health is the goal, prerequisite and result of sustainable development, its promotion is a re-quirement of humanity and part of responsible government policy (...). The challenges in the health sector are still huge."* In Central Asia, the prevalence of opioid use is twice as high as in Europe, in China there are almost up to 3–5 million opioid users, still a small number in relation to the total population, but an enormous problem for the healthcare system. There are too few offers for help. The staff is qualified and highly motivated, but consists al-most entirely of medical doctors – social work as a central component of the services (in Ger-many) is neither offered at university education nor in practice. The well-being of those affected also depends on the offers of help and the re-duction of stigmatization and marginalization. *Goal 4: quality education "Education is a human right – it empowers people to improve their political, social, cultural, and economic situation."* In post-Soviet Central Asia, as well as in China, high-quality education is an important socio-political concern. However, there are too few specific training opportunities for the prevention and treatment of addictions. *Goal 5: Gender equality* Gender equality and self-determination for all women and girls are a principle of German de-velopment policy. In Central Asia and China, women have equal rights under the constitu-tions, but still not in social reality, they earn less, they mostly have a double burden on family and work and only play a "minority role" at the political level. Medical professions and social work (except in Tajikistan) have a "female" dominance, but the management structures are male. *Goal: 10 Reduce inequality within and between countries* Social and economic inequality is a major challenge for the development of stability and well-being. Addiction is (also) a phenomenon of social inequalities and poverty, i.e. the proportion of people with social and economic problems among ad-dicted people is disproportionately high. *Goal 16: Promote peaceful and inclusive societies for sustainable development, give everyone access to justice and build effective, accountable and inclusive institutions at all levels.* Drug addiction had been and is still seen in both Central Asia and the People's Republic of China more as a *"social deviation"* problem than as a treatable disease; existing drug laws mean that many of those affected have to face (often long) prison terms and that the police and judiciary are still in the *learning phase* of a better cooperation with health and social services. This and the registration system promote the social exclusion of those affected. The program is compatible with the *"Central Asian Drug Action Program"*

(CADAP), which the EU will implement also in a planned 7th phase from 2020 to 2024. It is about "the establishment of functional and effective treatment and harm reduction programs based on EU and international standards (which) are essential to provide the best and cutting-edge health responses, programs and models to CA countries' populations. This output will focus on strengthening demand reduction models on the basis of best EU and international practices for harm re-duction, rehabilitation and social reintegration, and therapeutic communities." (Annual Action Document 2019 for the program in favour of the Central Asia region; July 2019). It is of central importance to support the training of social work in the Central Asian countries, which plays a central role in Europe and especially in Germany in the prevention and treatment of drug addiction and its health and social consequences. But social work as a means of reducing these problems is still in its infancy both in Central Asia and in China. Adequate job descriptions and job offers are still scarce, although the positive role of social work is now increasingly recognized at socio-political level. [45][43]

Acknowledgements

The article is based on the experiences of the DAAD exceed project SOL-ID: Social work and strengthening of NGOs in development cooperation to treat drug addiction; financed by the Federal Ministry of Economic Development and International Cooperation (BMZ), Germany and conducted by the Frankfurt University of Applied Sciences

---

43 45 The Frankfurt University of Applied Sciences has accumulated decades of competence in the training of social work in Department 4 "Social Work and Health" (Bachelor, also a course "Social Work: transnational" as well as the master's program "Addiction Therapy and Social Management in Addiction Help" and in practical research, in particular through numerous research projects by the project manager Prof. Dr. Stöver and the research stay of Dr. Ingo Ilja Michels from 2006 and 2008 in the PR China to accompany and support the establishment of an opiate substitution program including social work (especially with a pilot character in Shanghai). See: Michels I.I. (2007): *"Models of social work with drug users in Europe"*. Lectures at the East China University of Science & Technology (ECUST) Department of Social Work Institute of Ap-plied Sociology in cooperation with Fan Zhihai Fan and Dr. Xuesong He; Internal Report, Shanghai June 1st.

References

[1] Altice, F. L., Azbel, L., Stone, J., Brooks-Pollock, E., Smyrnov, P., Dvoriak, S., Taxman, F. S., El- Bassel, N., Martin, N. K., Booth, R., Stöver, H., Dolan, K., & Vickerman, P. (2016). The perfect storm: incarceration and the high-risk environment perpetuating transmission of HIV, hepatitis C virus, and tuberculosis in Eastern Europe and Central Asia. The Lancet, 388(10050), 1228- 1248. https://doi.org/10.1016/S0140-6736(16)30856- X

[2] Azbel, L., Rozanova, J., Michels, I., Altice, F. L., & Stöver, H. (2017). A qualitative assessment of an abstinence-oriented therapeutic community for prisoners with substance use disorders in Kyrgyzstan. Harm Reduction Journal, 14(1), 1-9. https://doi.org/10.1186/s12954-017-0168-8

[3] Azizov, U. (2017). Regional integration in Central Asia: From knowing-that to knowing-how. Journal of Eurasian Studies, 8(2), 123–135. https://doi.org/10.1016/j.euras.2017.02.002 Barnard, A. (2008). Values, Ethics and Professionalization: a Social Work History. In The Value Base of Social Work and Social Care (pp. 6–24). Bernays, S., Rhodes, T., & Jankovic Terźić, K. (2010). "You should be grateful to have medicines": Continued dependence, altering stigma and the HIV treatment experience in Serbia. AIDS Care – Psychological and Socio-Medical Aspects of AIDS/HIV, 22(1), 14–20. https://doi.org/10.1080/09540120903499220

[4] Borrmann St., Michel-Schwartze, B., Pankofer, S., Sagebiel, J., Spatscheck, C. (ed) (2016): Die Wissenschaft Soziale Arbeit im Diskurs Auseinandersetzungen mit den theoriebilden-den Grundlagen Sozialer Arbeit; Theorie, Forschung und Praxis der Sozialen Arbeit (The science of social work in discourse Discourse on the theoretical foundations of social work; Theory, research and practice of social work)

[5] Bobrova, N., Rughnikov, U., Neifeld, E., Rhodes, T., Alcorn, R., Kirichenko, S., & Power, R. (2008). Challenges in providing drug user treatment services in Russia: Providers' views. Sub-stance Use and Misuse, 43(12–13), 1770–1784. https://doi.org/10.1080/10826080802289291 Bobrova, N., Sarang, A., Stuikyte, R., & Lezhentsev, K. (2007). Obstacles in provision of anti-retroviral treatment to drug users in Central and Eastern Europe and Central Asia: A regional overview. International Journal of Drug Policy, 18(4), 313–318. https://doi.org/10.1016/j.drugpo.2007.01.015

[6] Brocato, J., & Wagner, E. F. (2003). Harm Re-duction: A social work practice model and social justice agenda. Health and Social Work, 28(2), 117–125. Burke, A. C., & Clapp, J. D. (1997). Ideology and Social Work Practice in Substance Abuse Settings. Social Work, 42(6), 552–562. http://www.ncbi.nlm.nih.gov/pubmed/9414633

[7] Cisaltina, M., & Dinis, S. N. (2013). Social Work Approaches for Substance-Use Treatment. The International Journal of Health, Wellness and Society, 2(2), 23–35

[8] Deutsche Gesellschaft für Soziale Arbeit in der Suchthilfe DGSAS (2016): Kompetenzprofil der Sozialen Arbeit in der Suchthilfe und Suchtprävention; Münster (German Society for Social Work in Addiction Help DGSAS (2016): Competence Profile of Social Work in Addiction Help and Addiction Prevention; Muenster)

[9] Demerath, L., & Alasuutari, P. (1996). Researching culture: Qualitative method and cultural studies. In Contemporary Sociology (1st ed., Vol. 25). SAGE Publication Ltd. https://doi.org/10.2307/2077614 Dickson-Swift, V., James, E. L., & Liamputtong, P. (2008). Undertaking sensitive research in the health and social sciences: Managing boundaries, emotions, and risks. Cambridge University Press. www.cambridge.org

[10] DiNitto, D. M., & McNeece, C. A. (2008). Addictions and social work practice. In Social Work: Issues and 19 Opportunities in a Challenging Profession (pp. 171–192). http://ovidsp.ovid.com/ovid-web. cgi?T=JS&PAGE=reference&D=psyc6&NEWS=N&AN=2008–03930- 008

[11] Dole, V. P., & Nyswander, M. (1965). A Medical Treatment for Diacetylmorphine (Heroin) Addiction: A Clinical Trial With Methadone Hydrochloride. JAMA: The Journal of the American Medical Association, 193(8), 646–650. https://doi.org/10.1001/jama.1965.0309008000 8002

[12] Domes, M., Sagebiel, J. (2016): Theorien als Medium der Indentitätsbildung; In: Die Wissenschaft Soziale Arbeit im Diskurs Auseinandersetzungen mit den theoriebildenden Grundlagen Sozialer Arbeit; Theorie, Forschung und Praxis der Sozialen Arbeit (Theories as a medium of identity formation; In: The Science of Social Work in Discourse Discourse on the theoretical foundations of social work; Theory, Research and Practice of Social Work)

[13] Dominelli, L. (2020). Personal reflections on 30 years of social work development in China. China Journal of Social Work, 1–8. https://doi.org/10.108 0/17525098.2020.175620 9 Glazer, S. (2006). Social support across cultures. International Journal of Intercultural Relations, 30(5), 605–622. https://doi.org /10.1016/j.ijintrel.2005.01.013 Gray, M., & Coates, J. (2010). "Indigenization" and knowledge development: Extending the de-bate. International Social Work, 53(5), 613–627. https://doi.org/10.1177/0020872810372160 Healy, L. M. (2008). Exploring the history of social work as a human rights profession. International Social Work, 51(6), 735–748. https://doi.org/10.1177/0020872808095247

[14] Farfiev, B. (2009). Historical roots of development of social help in the Central Asia. *Social Sciences In Uzbekistan, 1,* pp. 86–91

[15] Grebneva, I. (2006): Social work development in Kazakhstan. A ladder to a healthier nation; Inter-national Social Work 49(6): 819–823

[16] Hansjürgens, R. (2015): Soziale Arbeit in der ambulanten Suchthilfe. In: Konturen: Schwerpunktthema Ambulante Suchthilfe (Social work in outpatient addiction support. In: Contours: Focus on outpatient addiction help)

[17] Hauschildt, E. (1995): "Auf den richtigen Weg zwingen..." Trinkerfürsorge 1922 – 1945 ("Forcing them on the right path ..." Drinker Care 1922 – 1945)

[18] Healy, L.M. (2001) *International Social Work: Professional Action in an Interdependent World.* Oxford: Oxford University Press

[19] Hering, S., Münchmeier R. (2013): Geschichte der Sozialen Arbeit. Weinheim und Basel. ISBN 978–3–7799–14 (2013)46–4 (History of Social Work. Weinheim and Basel. ISBN 978–3- 7799–14 (2013) 46–4)

[20] Holleran-Steiker, L. (2016). Youth and sub-stance use: Prevention, intervention, and recovery. Lyceum Books, Inc.

[21] Hrovatic, D. (2020): Social work between the social policy and practice. The Slovenian case of social work theory for practice; in: Social Work in the XXI century: Domestic and International experience; Bishkek State University publication (СОЦИАЛЬНАЯ РАБОТА В XXI ВЕКЕ: ОТЕЧЕСТВЕННЫЙ И

[22] МЕЖДУ НАРОДНЫЙ ОПЫТ СОЦИАЛЬНАЯ РАБОТА В XXI ВЕКЕ: ОТЕЧЕСТВЕННЫЙ И

[23] М Е Ж Д У Н А Р О Д Н Ы Й ОПЫТ; Бишкек) (СОЦИАЛДЫК КЫЗМАТ XXI КЫЛЫМДА: АТА- МЕКЕНДИК ЖАНА ЭЛ АРАЛЫК ТАЖРЫЙБА; Бишкек)

[24] InBeAIDS. (2020). Prevention of infectious dis-eases and treatment of HIV/ AIDS and hepatitis among injecting drug users in Central Asia and the contribution of social work to the services for drug using people (InBeAIDS). Report: Frankfurt am Main and Bishkek. International Network of People Who Use Drugs (INPUD) and Asian Network of People Who Use Drugs (ANPUD). (2019). Words matter! Language statement and reference guide. https://doi.org/ 10.1016/j.dru-galcdep. 2006.10.014.INPUD

[25] International Federation of Social Workers (IFSW) (2000) 'Definition of Social Work'. Available online at: http://www.ifsw.org

[26] Jolley, E., Rhodes, T., Platt, L., Hope, V., Latypov, A., Donoghoe, M., & Wilson, D. (2012). HIV among people who inject drugs in Central and Eastern Europe and Central Asia: A systematic review with implications for policy. BMJ Open, 2(5). https://doi.org/10.1136/bmjopen-2012-001465 Klein, A. (2008). Drugs and the World. Reaktion Books

[27] Klein, M. (1999). Praxisfeld Suchthilfe [The practice of addiction treatment]. In: Badry, E., Buchka, M. & Knapp, R. (ed). Pädagogik. Grundlagen und Arbeitsfelder. Neuwied: Luchterhand, 495 – 505.

[28] Koch, M. (2017): Unterschiede zwischen der sozialen Arbeit in der BRD und der DDR; München https://www.grin.com/documents/436094 (Differences between social work in the FRG and the GDR; Munich https://www.grin.com/d ocuments/436094)

[29] Laging, M. (2018): Soziale Arbeit in der Suchthilfe: Grundlagen – Konzepte – Methoden (Grundwissen Soziale Arbeit, Band 28) (Social work in addiction support: Basics – Concepts – Methods (Basic Knowledge of Social Work, Volume 28)

[30] Manual of the postgraduate master's course Addiction therapy and social management in addiction support Master of Arts (M.A.) (2016): Frankfurt University of Applied Sciences

[31] Meng, Q., Gray, M., Bradt, L. (2021): A critical review of Chinese and international social work: Walking a tightrope between local and global standards; In: International Journal of Social Work, 8 January *doi.org/ 10.1177/0020872820963424*

[32] McInnes, A. (2012). Why should they listen to me? Developing social work education and social work in Tajikistan. International Social Work, 56(5), 674–689. https://doi.org/10.1177/0020872812440716

[33] Michels, I. I., Keizer, B., Trautmann, F., Stöver, H., & Robelló, E. (2017). Improvement of Treatment of Drug use Disorders in Central Asia the contribution of the EU Central Asia Drug Action Programme (CADAP). Journal of Addiction Medicine and Therapy, 5(1), 1–14.

[34] Michels, I. I., & Stöver, H. (2012). Harm reduction – From a conceptual framework to practical experience: The example of Germany Substance Use and Misuse, 47(8–9), 910–922. https://doi.org/10.3109/10826084.2012.663281

[35] Michels, I. I., Stöver, H.; Aizberg, O. and Boltaev, A. (2020): Opioid Agonist Treatment for Opioid Use Disorder patients in Central Asia; Heroin Addiction and Related Clinical Problems, March

[36] Ministry of Labour and Social Protection of population of the Republic of Kazakhstan. (2020): virtually *International Social Workers Online Forum*, August 12, Nur Sultan

[37] Ministry of Civil Affairs PRC. (2012). Shehuigongzuo zhuanye rencai duiwu jianshe zhongzhangqi guihua 20 (2011–2020nian) [The Middle-to-long Term Development Plan for Social Work Professionals 2011 – 2020]. http://jnjd.mca.g ov.cn/arti-cle/zyjd/zczx/201301/20130100406268.shtml

[38] Museva N. (2012): Influence of International ex-perience on the development of Social work in Kyrgyzstan; Bishkek (Мусаева Н. (2012): ВЛИЯНИЕ МЕЖДУНАРОДНОГО ОПЫТА НА РАЗВИТИЕ СОЦИАЛЬНОЙ РАБОТЫ В КЫРГЫЗСТАНЕ; г. Бишкек)

[39] Musaeva N. (2012): Social Work as an object of philosophical analysis (Социальная работа как объект философского анализа). Dissertation published on portal of the National Electronic Library of the National Academy of Sciences of the Kyrgyz Republic, Institute of Philosophy and political and legal studies; Bishkek [40] Nikku, B. R. (2015). International Social Work. In International Encyclopedia of the Social & Behavioural Sciences: Second Edition (Second Edi, Vol. 12). Elsevier. https://doi.org/10.1016/B978-0-08- 097086-8.28048 – 3

[41] Nöthling C. (2009): Soziale Arbeit und Soziale Bewegungen in der DDR; in: Leonie Wagner: Soziale Arbeit und Soziale Bewegungen, 207–230 (Social work and social movements in the GDR; in: Leonie Wagner: Social Work and Social Movements)

[42] Room, R. (2005). Stigma, social inequality and alcohol and drug use. Drug and Alcohol Review, 24(2), 143–155. https://doi.org/10.1080/09595230500102 434 Schwartz, S. H. (1994). Beyond individual-ism/collectivism: {New} cultural dimensions of values. In Individualism and collectivism: {Theory}, method, and applications (pp. 85–119). https://doi.org/10.1017/CBO9781107415324.00 4 Shaw, I. (2008). Ethics and the practice of qualitative research. Qualitative Social Work, 7(4), 400–414. https://doi.org/10.1177/1473325008097137

[43] Sagebiel, J. (2016): Soziale Arbeit als normative Handlungstheorie. Was ist Soziale Arbeit? Was sind soziale Probleme? In: Konzepte der Sozialpädagogik; sozialpädagogische Impulse; 4/2016; S. 31 – 33 (Social work as a normative theory of action. What is social work? What are social problems? In: Concepts of Social Pedagogy; socio-educational impulses; 4/2016; P.31 – 33)

[44] Sagebiel, J. (2017): Macht und Ohnmacht der Sozialen Arbeit. In: Domes, Michael/Eming, Knut (Hg.): Soziale Arbeit – Perspektiven einer selbstbewussten Disziplin und Profession; S. 63–82 (Power and impotence of social work. In: Domes, Michael / Eming, Knut (ed.): Social work – perspectives of a self-confident discipline and profession; Pp. 63–82)

[45] Sherraden, M., Yuen-Tsang, A. W. K., Wang, S., Khinduka, S., Zou, L., Deng, S., Gao, J., Ku, B. H. B., Huang, J., Sherraden, M., & Morrow- Howell, N. (2020). Re-emergence of social work in modern China: A perspective by Chinese and U.S. partners. China Journal of Social Work, 13(1), 40–54. https://doi.o rg/10.1080/17525098.2020.173253_4

[46] Stöver, H. (2009). South Caucasus anti-drug (SCAD) programme (Phase V). https://doi.org/10.2174/138920312803582960

[47] Sheripkanova, A. (Association of Social Work Alumni in the Kyrgyz Republic) (2020): Social work education in Kyrgyzstan: challenges and achievements

[48] Stöver, H., Deimel, D., & Hösselbarth, S. (2017). Social work and support of people who use drugs in Germany. In Getting to Zero: Global So-cial Work Responds to HIV (pp. 101–126).

[49] Stöver, H., Jamin, D., Michels, I. I., Knorr, B., Keppler, K., & Deimel, D. (2019). Opioid substitution therapy for people living in German prisons – inequality compared with civic sector. Harm Reduction Journal, 16(1), 1–9. https://doi.org/10.1186/s12954-019-0340-4

[50] Stöver, H. (2012): Konzepte und Arbeits-methoden der Sozialen Arbeit in der Suchthilfe. In: Suchttherapie 13 (04), S. 162–166 (Concepts and working methods of social work in addiction help. In: Suchttherapie 13 (04), pp. 162–166)

[51] Sultan, A., & Mažeikienė, N. (2019). Living with HIV in post-Soviet states: Rejecting individual stigma through social activism. International Social Work. https://doi.org/10.1177/0020872819858746

[52] Tappan C. (2012): Social Work on the Silk Road. The New Social Worker, Vol. 19, No. 2

[53] Thombs, D. L., & Osborn, C. J. (2013). Introduction to addictive behaviors (4th ed.). In Introduction to addictive behaviors (4th ed.). Guilford Press.

[54] Tulchinsky, T. H., & Varavikova, E. A. (1996). Addressing the epidemiologic transition in the former Soviet Union: Strategies for health system and public health reform in Russia. Ameri-can Journal of Public Health, 86(3), 313–320. https://doi.org/10.2105/AJPH.86.3.313 UN Joint Programme on HIV/AIDS (UNAIDS). (2014). The gap report. United Nations Human Rights Declara-tion, 2 (1948). https://www.ohchr.org/EN/UDHR/Docu-ments/ UDHR_Trans-lations/eng.pdf United Nations Department of Economic and Social Affairs. (2020). Achieving SDGs in the wake of COVID-19: Scenarios for policymakers. In Sustainable Development Outlook. https://doi.org/10.18356/7a3ee84a-en 21 UNODC. (2010). Accessibility of HIV Prevention, Treatment and Care Services for People who Use Drugs and Incarcerated People in Azerbaijan, Kazakhstan, Kyrgyzstan, Tajikistan, Turkmenistan and Uzbekistan: Legislative and policy analysis and recommendations for reform.

[55] Xu, H., Zeng, Y., & Anderson, A. F. (2005). Chinese NGOs in action against HIV/AIDS. Cell Re-search, 15(11–12), 914–918. https://doi.org/10.1038/sj.cr.72 90368 Yuan, Y., He, X., & Duan, W. (2020). A reflection on the current China social work education in the com-bat with COVID-19. Social Work Education, 00(00), 1–8. https://doi.org/10.1080/02615479.2020.182163 7

[56] Xiong, Y. & Wang, S.(2007) : Development of Social Work Education in China in the Context of New Policy Initiatives: Issues and Challenges; Social Work Education Vol. 26, No. 6, September 2007, pp. 560–572

[57] Yergaliyeva A. (2019): Kazakh social workers to start adaptation course for children returned from Iraq; in: International, 28 November; reprint in Astana Times from 16 January 2021

[58] Yuen-Tsang, A., Ku, B., & Ku, B. (2016). A Journey of a Thousand Miles begins with One Step: The Development of Culturally Relevant Social Work Education and Fieldwork Practice in China. In Indigenous Social Work around the World: Towards Culturally Relevant Education and Practice (pp. 205–218). Routledge. https://doi.org/10.4324/9781315588360-25

[59] Zinovieva, V. I., & Naumova, N. I. (2017). Development of the specialty "Social Work" in the educational system of Kazakhstan. Vestnik Tomskogo Gosudarstvennogo Universiteta, 425, 74–77. https://doi.org/10.17223/15617793/425/9

[60] Zhang, W. (2009): Soziale Arbeit in China – Einführung in die Rahmenbe-dingungen, die Struktur und den Stand; Forum für Erziehungshilfen 109–112 (ISSN 0947–8957) (Social work in China – introduction to the framework, structure and status; Forum for Educational Aids 109–112 (ISSN 0947–8957)

Authors

Ingo Ilja Michels, Ph.D., is sociologist and advisor for treatment of drug dependence. Since 2010, he was Project Leader of the EU Central Asia Drug Action Programme (CADAP), since 2020 he is the International Scientific Coordinator of the DAAD project "Social work and strengthening NGOs in development cooperation to treat drug addiction" (SOLID) of the Frankfurt University of Applied Sciences. He worked in psychiatric clinic with drug dependent heroin user, as Head of the Drugs and Prison projects department of the German AIDS-Hilfe in Berlin, as Drug Commissioner of the Federal State of Bremen in northern Germany, and as Head of the Office of the Federal Drug Commissioner within the Federal Ministry of Health in Berlin. He is freelance advisor for drug services in PR China in Beijing and Shanghai and Guest Professor at the Department of Sociology/Social Work of the East China University of Science and Technology (ECUST), Shanghai. He is author of several articles on prevention and treatment of drug dependents and on drug policy in International Journals on Substance Use.

Heino Stöver, Ph.D., is social scientist and Professor of Social Scientific Addiction Research, Faculty of Health and Social Work at the University of Applied Sciences in Frankfurt, Germany. since 2020 he is the Project Director of the DAAD project "Social work and strengthening NGOs in development cooperation to treat drug addiction" (SOLID) of the Frankfurt University of Applied Sciences Since 1987, he is director of the Archive and Documentation Centre for Drug Literature and Research at the University of Bremen (www.archido.de), the Bremen Institute for Drug Research ISDRO), and the "Institute of Addiction Research of the University of Applied Sciences in Frankfurt am Main" (www.isff.de). Main fields of his research and project development expertise are health promotion for vulnerable groups, drug services, prisons, and related health issues (especially HIV/AIDS, Hepatitis C, and drug dependence). Consultant for the European Commission, United Nations Office on Drugs and Crime (UNODC), WHO, European Monitoring Centre for Drugs and Drug Addiction (EMCDDA), International Committee of the Red Cross (ICRC), and Open Society Institute (OSI) in various contexts. He has published several articles in international journals and books on preventing and treating infectious diseases adequately (HIV/AIDS, hepatitis, STIs, and TB), opioid substitution programs.

Baigabylov N.O., PhD in Sociology, Associate Professor and Head of the Department of Sociology of L.N. Gumilyov ENU (L. N. Gumilyov **Eurasian National University** (**ENU**), Research interests: ethnosociology, sociology of migration, social work. In 2012–2013, he completed a scientific internship at the Istanbul University at the Department of Sociology, and at the Scientific Research Center of the Turkic World in Istanbul (Turkey), 2014 – advanced training courses in sociology at the University of Nijmegen (Netherlands). In the 2018–2019 academic year, he completed a postdoctoral program at the Institute of Sociology of Gazi University (Ankara, Turkey); 2019 – participated in seminars at the Migration Research Center (Ankara, Turkey); 2019 – visiting researcher at the Yildirim Beyazit University Migration Center (Ankara, Turkey). Baigabylov N.O. He is the Deputy Editor-in-Chief of the scientific journal "Bulletin of the Eurasian National University. L.N. Gumilyov (direction – Sociology), from 2017 to the present time as a member of the editorial board of the journal "Society & Security Insights" (Altai State University, Russia), in 2015 – as a member of the editorial board of the Global Dialogue Magazine International Sociological Association.He has experience in the implementation of grant projects, international research. From 2017–2018, 2020–2021 was the national coordinator of joint projects of L.N. Gumilyov ENU and the United Nations Children's Fund (UNICEF) in the field of social protection and support for families with children.Author of 76 scientific publications, 11 intellectual property copyright certificates, including 7 in peer-reviewed scientific publications indexed in the Scopus database. https://www.scopus.com/authid/detail.uri?authorId=55933633 600.

Jarkyn Shadymanova is an associate professor at the Bishkek State University and American University of Central Asia. She holds a PhD degree in Sociology. Her research interests include qualitative and quantitative research methods, social work, sociology of deviation and sustainable consumption issues gender studies. She was a postdoctoral researcher at the Sociology Consumption and Household Group, Wageningen University and Department of Anthropology, University of Amsterdam. Jarkyn is an author and co-author of numerous articles in peer-reviewed journals and book chapters on social issues. Jarkyn received several fellowship grants such as of The Global Dialogues & Women's Empowerment in Eurasian Contexts Feminist Mentoring (WEF) Fellowship, IGS, LMH, Oxford University, 2018. 'Gendering the Youth: Representations of Gender in Contemporary Kyrgyzstan Media' Junior Fellowship Central Asia Research and Training Initiative, OSI, 2006- 2008; and "Building Academic and Teaching Excellence in the Discipline of Sociology in Central Asia" ReSET, CARC, Almaty, Kazakhstan, HESP, OSI 2003–2006.

Nurgul Musaeva is Associate Professor of Psychology since and Philosophical Sciences (specializing in Social Philosophy at Bishkek State University (BSU) named after K. Karasayev, socio-psychological faculty // specialist in social work, with additional qualification "Psychologist-practitioner". She is Scientific Coordinator of the DAAAD exceed SOLID project in cooperation with Frankfurt University of Applied Sciences. From 2012 – 2015 she worked at "Resource department" for advanced training of social pedagogues and social workers at the Chui regional rehabilitation center for children with disabilities "Maksat". From 2004 – to the present she is Associate Professor of the Department of Management, Social and Information Technologies of the Institute of Continuous and Distance Education. She is teaching "Family-oriented approach in social work", "Social work in Kyrgyzstan", "History of social work", "Social pedagogy", "Psychology of personality", "Social psychology", "Fundamentals of psychological consulting in social work", "Educational psychology", "Legal support in social work", "Social innovations", "Methodology of dissertation research", etc. She is managing of pedagogical practices of students and undergraduates, graduate qualification works and master's theses.

Akhatjon Nasullaev, PhD, had been Vice-rector for International cooperation at Bukhara state medical institute. He obtained his bachelor degree in international relations from the University of World Economy and Diplomacy, Uzbekistan in 2012. During 2012–2024, he studied at Master's program in Cooperation and Development at the University of Pavla Institute of Advanced Studies, Italy. In 2014 – 2015, he works as a senior methodologist, chief methodologist and senior teacher at the Academy of Public Administration under the President of the Republic of Uzbekistan. In 2015–2019 he studied in PhD program "Management, finance and law for business" at Carlo Cattaneo University, Italy. During 2018–2019, he studied at the Tallin University of Technology in Estonia, the University of Bordeaux in France and the Prague University of Economics in Czech Republic as a visiting PhD student. In 2019, hr received a PhD degree in Italy, successfully defending a doctoral dissertation in management. At this moment Akhatjon Nasullaev worked as Post-Doc researcher of the DAAD exceed project "Social Work and strengthening of NGOs in development cooperation to treat drug addiction – SOLID". He will conduct research on strengthening international cooperation to treat drug addiction during this project.

Hang Su has been engaged since 2011 in the basic and clinical research of drug dependence and substance addiction, and learn knowledge about addiction medicine, psychology, epidemiology and sociology. Hang Su now is a postdoctor in Shanghai Mental Health Center, majoring in psychiatry and mental health. Most of the time, Hang Su communicate with substance users in drug rehabilitation institutions and rehabilitation communities to understand their physical, mental state and social needs. At present, Hang Su is doing research focusing on the treatment of amphetamine type stimulants and opioids addiction from several aspects: behavior, electrophysiology, molecular biology, neuroimaging,etc.